# Filipino
## martial art anthology

An Anthology of Articles from the *Journal of Asian Martial Arts*

Compiled by Michael A. DeMarco, M.A.

**Disclaimer**
Please note that the authors and publisher of this book are not responsible in any manner whatsoever for any injury that may result from practicing the techniques and/or following the instructions given within. Since the physical activities described herein may be too strenuous in nature for some readers to engage in safely, it is essential that a physician be consulted prior to training.

**All Rights Reserved**
No part of this publication, including illustrations, may be reproduced or utilized in any form or by any means, electronic or mechanical, including photocopying, recording, or by any information storage and retrieval system (beyond that copying permitted by sections 107 and 108 of the US Copyright Law and except by reviewers for the public press), without written permission from Via Media Publishing Company.

**Warning:** Any unauthorized act in relation to a copyright work may result in both a civil claim for damages and criminal prosecution.

Copyright © 2017
by Via Media Publishing Company
941 Calle Mejia #822, Santa Fe, NM 87501 USA

Articles in this anthology were originally published in the *Journal of Asian Martial Arts* and the book, *Asian Martial Arts: Constructive Thoughts & Practical Applications*. Listed according to the table of contents for this anthology:

Wiley M. (1994), Vol. 3 No. 2, pp. 72-86
Wiley M. (1996), Vol. 5 No. 3, pp. 20-39
Dowd, S. (1997), Vol. 6 No. 2, pp. 70-79
Wiley M. (1997), Vol. 6 No. 3, pp. 96-107
Soderholm, M. (2004), Vol. 13 No. 1, pp. 56-63
Hobart, P. (2007), Vol. 16 No. 1, pp. 54-63
Macaraeg, R. (2009), Vol. 18 No. 3, pp. 40-49
Smith, K. (2012), In *Asian Martial Arts: Constructive Thoughts & Practical Applications*, pp. 124-127

Book and cover design
by Via Media Publishing Company
Edited by Michael A. DeMarco, M.A.

## Cover illustration

Master of Modern Arnis, Ken Smith demonstrates a technique.
http://modernarnisacademy.com
Background: Taming shield courtesy of the
University of Pennsylvania Museum (neg. #S4-141889).

ISBN 978-1-893765-44-3

www.viamediapublishing.com

# contents

iv **Preface**
by Michael DeMarco, M.A.

## CHAPTERS

1 **Classical Eskrima:**
**The Evolution and Etymology of a Filipino Fencing Form**
by Mark V. Wiley, B.S.

20 **The Classification and Ethos of Filipino Martial Traditions**
by Mark V. Wiley, B.S.

43 **Showing the Forms of Filipino Kuntaw Lima-Lima**
by Steven K. Dowd

56 **Philippine Arms & Armor in the University of Pennsylvania Museum of Archaeology and Anthropology**
by Mark V. Wiley, B.S.

70 **The Art of Conversation:**
**Random Flow Training in Visayan Corto Kadena Eskrima**
by Majia Soderholm, B.Sc.

83 **Remy Presas Remembered:**
**A Perspective on Life in the Martial Arts**
by Peter Hobart, J.D.

94 **Pirates of the Philippines: A Critical Thinking Exercise**
by Ruel A. Macaraeg, M.A., J.D.

107 **A Few Favored Modern Arnis Techniques**
by Ken Smith

111 **Index**

# preface

There has been a lack of reliable academic studies regarding Filipino martial arts (FMA) that have uniquely developed in the Philippine archipelago. This anthology assembles pioneering scholarly materials valuable for any interested in the Filipino combatives, as well as chapters specifically on the practice.

Mark Wiley stands out as a leading scholar/practitioner of the Filipino arts. This book contains three chapters by him. In the first, he conducted linguistic and historical research to present the developmental background of the ancient Filipino kali and European fencing systems, thus illuminating the evolution of classical eskrima.

In chapter two, Wiley attempts to classify Filipino martial arts and explore the ethos of Filipino martial culture by deriving information directly from the contemporary grandmasters who have maintained an oral transmission of information concerning the evolution and development of their respective martial systems.

Part of Wiley's research also led him to seek out special repositories of artifacts. Museums collections rarely include much on Southeast Asian weapons. University of Pennsylvania Museum of Archaeology and Anthropology has nearly 1,000 martial artifacts in storerooms from the Philippines, including swords, knives, spears, shields, helmets, and armor discussed in Wiley's third chapter.

On a practical side, Steven Dowd presents the art of Carlita Lañada who studied martial arts as passed down within his own family in the Philippines. He calls his rendition Kuntaw Lima-Lima, an art whose techniques are reminiscent of Okinawan karate styles, with hints of Chinese gongfu. Presented are the underlying principles, and a *sayawan* (form) with applications.

Majia Soderholm's chapter is about Visayan Corto Kadena Eskrima and some of its concepts and training methods with regard to free-sparring with swords. It is a Filipino martial system encompassing empty-hand and non-bladed and bladed weapons.

Peter Hobart presents a wonderful tribute to Remy Presas, the founder of Modern Arnis. This retrospective is comprised of the stories and memories of many of those who knew him. Topics include Presas' theory and practice of arnis, such as importance of flow, and memories of his last seminar.

The chapter by Ruel Macaraeg dives into the topic of piracy in the Philippines. His study reconstructs the pirates' martial practices through comparative historical analysis of their weapons, costume, and organization in order to draw conclusions about their relationship to martial cultures in the Philippines and across the region.

In the final chapter, Ken Smith discusses a few of his favorite techniques from Modern Arnis. His insights—as well as the information found in the previous chapters—contribute to the academic understanding of Filipino martial traditions as well as the actual practice of kali, escrima, and arnis. We hope you'll enjoy the reading.

Michael A. DeMarco, Publisher
Santa Fe, New Mexico
February 2017

chapter 1

# Classical Eskrima:
## The Evolution and Etymology of a Filipino Fencing Form

by Mark V. Wiley, B.S.

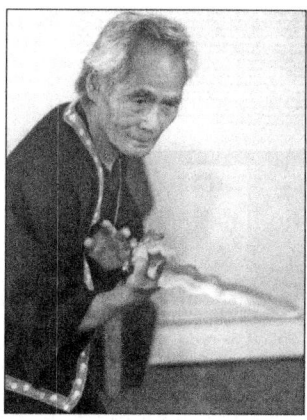

Florendo M. Visitacion, founder of Vee Arnis-Jitsu.
*Photograph courtesy of Rey Galang.*

Since its pre-Hispanic times, the martial culture of the Philippines has continued to evolve. The native wrestling art of *buno* (tag.)* and the sword-based fighting arts of *kali* (tag.; derived from *kalis*, tag., *sabre*, sword)[1] were at one time earnestly practiced in the Philippines as a means of defending one's land against attacks from the inhabitants of neighboring islands. Although Indonesian *pencak-silat* (ind.) and Malaysian *langka-silat* (ind.) predate kali as a fighting art in the Philippines,[2] they continue to maintain their respective identities in the republic's Muslim areas of Mindanao, Palawan, and the Sulu Archipelago. Hence, the art of kali, transferred to the island of Panay during the twelfth century, was, perhaps, the first identifiable, standardized system of combat to have developed in the Philippines. The art was practiced throughout the archipelago until the sixteenth century when Ferdinand Magellan unexpectedly docked off the coast of Samar Island. Although Magellan died in 1521 during the battle of Mactan, this rediscovery of the Philippines[3] led to 333 years of repressive Spanish domination in the Philippines' northern island of Luzon and central island cluster, the Visayas.

*See language abbreviation reference chart on page 16.

During the time of Spanish domination (1565-1896), Philippine martial culture was banned. The arts of kali, however, were preserved by way of the *komedya* (span.) plays, also known as the *moro-moro* (span.), *duplo* (vis.) and *arakyo* (tag.). In time the Spanish felt comfortable in their new territory and opened the ports of Manila Bay to world trade in 1834. Tensions had lessened to such a degree that compliant wealthy Filipinos were permitted to receive academic training in Europe. By that time the ancient arts of kali had declined and were relegated to simple folklore in these Spanish-dominated regions. It was the newly educated Filipino who brought back to the Philippines various techniques of European sword play. The inhabitants of Luzon and the Visayas then integrated this Occidental fencing form with what they had retained over the centuries of their ancestral kali forms. This integration of technique and principles evolved into a Filipino fencing form of single-stick, double-stick, and sword-and-dagger fencing that the Spanish termed *eskrima* (tag.; derived from *esgrima*, span., art of fencing) in the Visayas and *arnis* (tag.; derived from *arnés*, span., harness, decorative trappings; used by the moro-moro actors) on the island of Luzon.

In my attempt to better understand the evolution of classical eskrima, I conducted research into the developmental background of the ancient Filipino kali and European fencing systems. In presenting this evidence, I discuss their mutual effect on the more contemporary Filipino fencing form. In addition, I researched the etymology of the term "eskrima" with the hope that additional light would be shed on the origin of this art form. One can better appreciate the nature of this Filipino fencing form when the respective contributions of the Southeast Asian and European combat arts are traced.

**Legends of Pre-Hispanic Philippines**

It is generally believed that the Negrito, a pygmy tribe which hailed from Central Asia, were the first inhabitants of the Philippines. They presumably entered the islands by foot in search of food, travelling across two now-sunken land-bridges that connected Palawan to Borneo and the Celebes to Mindanao (Zaide, 1979). The Negrito brought to the archipelago skills in the use of the *sumpit* (tag., blow gun) and the *panà* (tag., bow and arrow), the points of which were covered with a poison made of various plant saps.

After the submersion of the land-bridges, Indonesians travelled to the Philippines in small boats (Scott, 1984). Arriving sometime between 3000 and 4000 B.C.E., they introduced the honed-edged weapons of the stone dagger, stone-tipped spear, and the hand-held shield. The first of three Malay migrations were arriving in the Philippines around 200 B.C.E. These head-hunting Malays became the ancestors of the Bontok, Ilongot, and

Tingguisan peoples of northern Luzon.

The second migratory wave spanned approximately thirteen centuries (100 C.E.-1400) and was responsible for introducing the ancient *baybayin* alphabet to the Philippines.[4] Legends of the thirteenth century, recorded in the *Maragtas*,[5] hold that ten *datus* (tag., tribal chieftains) fled their homeland of Borneo—running from the cruel Sultan Makatunaw—and settled on Panay Island, Philippines. On their arrival, Datu Puti, their leader and former prime minister of Makatunaw, bartered with the *Ati* (Negrito) natives for the purchase of Panay's lowlands to effect the establishment of a peaceful Malay-Bornean settlement. They were at once greeted with kindness by the Ati natives who agreed to sell the land for a mere gold headdress, necklace, and basin. The culmination of this agreement included a celebration feast during which the Negritos engaged in the *ati-ati* (festival dance) and the *sinulog* (vis., war dance).

It was on Panay that the datus established the *bothoan* (bicol), a legendary school where future tribal leaders of Panay were taught the skills of weaponry along with academics (Draeger and Smith, 1980; Marinas, 1986; Maliszewski, 1992b). It was on Panay that the Philippine art of kali was structured and developed. At that time and even among some southern Philippine systems found today, the art of kali was virtually indistinguishable from its Malaysian and Indonesian silat precursors.[6] These Malays are the ancestors of the modern-day Tagalogs, Bicols, Ilokanos, and Visayans.

Raymond Tobosa, founder of Tobosa Kau/Eskrima.
*Photograph courtesy of Toby Tobosa.*

The final Malay migration, which occurred during the thirteenth to fifteenth centuries, consisted of the Muslim Malays who are responsible for introducing the Islamic faith to the Philippine natives of Mindanao and the Sulu Archipelago.[7] These Malay immigrants (commonly called Moros) brought iron to the Philippines through the transplantation of the *kalis* (tag., sword), *balaniw* (tag., dagger), *sibcit* (tag., spear), and *lantaka* (tag., brass cannon) (Zaide, 1979).

In 1800, Don Baltazar Gonzales wrote his book, *De Los Delitos* (*Of the Crimes*), crediting Datu Mangal with bringing the art of kali to Mactan Island during the fifteenth century; *Sri* (skt., chief) Bataugong and his son Sri Bantug Lamay are credited with bringing the art to the island of Cebu. Through constant struggle and wars with neighboring islands, *Raja* (skt., king) Lapu Lapu, the son of Datu Mangal, developed a personalized system of kali he called *pangamut* (tag.). In the sixteenth century Lapu Lapu and Raja Humabon, the son of Sri Bantug Lamay, began to quarrel. A battle seemed imminent as Lapu Lapu accused Humabon of wrongfully taking land that belonged to his father. This battle, however, was never to take place as the Philippines was unexpectedly visited by the Spanish expedition headed by a Portuguese explorer named Ferdinand Magellan.

It was the initial Spanish discovery by Magellan and Miguel Lopez de Legaspi's subsequent colonization of the Philippines in 1565 which eventually forced the Filipinos to adopt a new way of life steeped in Christian values and European customs. The pressures of the Spanish invaders and their conquistadors temporarily halted the further development of kali on Luzon and the Visayas. However, it was the freedom-loving Moros of the southern Philippines, who have never been conquered, that are responsible for evolving the art of kali. They had also practiced and preserved their royal ancestral martial arts of *kuntao* (chin.), which originates in China and was further developed in Indonesia, and silat, which originates in Indonesia and Malaysia. Ironically, it was the Spanish methods of maneuvering the rapier and dagger which led to the evolution of eskrima, the art employed in 1898 by the *I* (tag.; members of the *katipunan*; tag., society, association)[8] in their revolution against Spain.

**The Etymology of Eskrima**

The derivation of the Filipino term eskrima is commonly believed to have come from the Spanish word *esgrima* (fencing). Further evidence, however, indicates that the word was also used in medieval literature. Hence, cognates of the term eskrima appear in all of the major romance languages (see Table 1).

**TABLE 1** **Escrima Cognates of Major Romance Languages**

| Language | Word | Meaning |
|---|---|---|
| Spanish | *esgrima* | fencing |
| Portuguese | *esgrima* | fencing |
| Italian | *scherma* | fencing |
| Romanian | *scrima* | fencing |
| French | *escrime* | fencing |

The minor romance languages, including Provincial, Catalan, and Romanch, also use a similar term. Therefore, it is possible that its origin is Latin. An investigation of the Latin use of this word, however, yielded surprising results. Words with similar meaning, such as "to fence," "to defend," and "sword," had no comparable cognate; in addition, no homophone could be found (see Table 2).

**TABLE 2** **Latin Words with Similar Meaning But Not Apparent Cognates**

| Language | Word | Meaning |
|---|---|---|
| Latin | *baruere* | to fence |
|  | *velitore* | to skirmish |
|  | *confligo* | to skirmish |
|  | *velitatio* | skirmish (n.) |
|  | *leve proelium* | skirmish (n.) |
|  | *defendere* | to defend |
|  | *gladius* | sword |

Further investigation of the term indicated several words with similar phonetics and semantic value such as in Old High German (spoken prior to 1100 C.E.), Old French (spoken prior to 1500 C.E.), and in Old English (spoken from 1150-1474 C.E.) (see Table 3).

**TABLE 3** **Escrima Cognates with Similar Phonetic and Semantic Value**

| Language | Word | Meaning |
|---|---|---|
| Old High German | *skirm* | to skirmish |
| Old French | *skirmiss* | to skirmish |
|  | *eskirmir* | to skirmish |
|  | *scaramouche* | to skirmish |
| Middle English | *scarmouche* | to skirmish |
|  | *skirmysshe* | to skirmish |

Inasmuch as the word *eskirmir* appears in Old French, it is further likely that its origin is Old Latin. Additional support for the Latin origin of the term is provided by the fact that as the area we once knew as West Germany (language = Old High German) was repeatedly invaded, conquered, and hence ruled by the Romans (Sinnigen and Boak, 1977). It is not unlikely, therefore, that the term was assimilated into the Germanic language. History also indicates that the Celts once ruled these areas (e.g., Spain, Italy, Greece, Turkey) prior to their conquest by the Roman Empire. The Romans conquered these regions around 70 C.E. (McKay, et al., 1991). The investigation of a Germanic connection (i.e., German, Swedish, Dutch, Danish, Icelandic) also resulted in some interesting findings (see Table 4).

**TABLE 4    Eskrima Cognates with a Germanic Connection**

| Language | Word | Meaning |
|---|---|---|
| Dutch | scherman | to fence |
| Swedish | skramma | to frighten |
|  | skrama | to scare |

Investigation of the older Germanic languages (precursors to Modern German, Dutch, Swedish) also uncovered the use of a term similar to eskrima (see Table 5).

**TABLE 5    Eskrima Cognates of Older Germanic Languages**

| Language | Word | Meaning |
|---|---|---|
| Old High German | skirm | to skirmish |
|  | scriman | to defend |
|  | scirman | to defend |
| Old English | scremman | to impede |
| Old Norse s | krymir | (mythological giant) |

Between 250 and 550 C.E., there was significant passage of the Germanic peoples, particularly the Goths, into the domain of the Roman Empire. The Teutons, Ostrogoths, and the Visigoths (old Germanic tribes) raided and in some cases settled in parts of this Empire. The Goths invaded Dacia (Romania) in 214 C.E. and then Thrace (Bulgaria), from 251 to 269 C.E. (Sinnigen and Boak, 1977; McKay, et al., 1991). Thus, the fourth-century Germans dominated the Romans, a situation which afforded ample opportunity for cross-lingual exchange. And so, the introduction into the Germanic languages of a word similar to "eskrima" (see Tables 1-5) quite possibly took place during these times. And the fencing form associated with such a term may also have evolved through similar cross-cultural exchanges.

## European Fencing Systems

During the fifteenth century, Europe saw a rise in fencing interest and consequently in the number of fencing academies. Even with this new found interest, the instructors of fencing were initially considered untrustworthy vagabonds. This attitude toward the fencing master and his art form is perhaps what kept those gentlemen of higher intellect from actively pursuing the art and aiding its further conceptual and practical development (Wise, 1971).[9] Conversely, Italy, Germany, and Spain saw the rise of the fencing master's place in society as he could openly instruct in his method of sword play. Moreover, he was looked upon as a man of honor, as noted by Nadi (1943: 5):

> Because of its origin, fencing should be the social sport par excellence ... In the past, the 'Master of Fence' belonged to a select class. He had to. No peasant mannerism could possibly be tolerated among the aristocracy he was privileged to teach, and as master of the art upon which life itself depended, he enjoyed all the prestige that went with it.

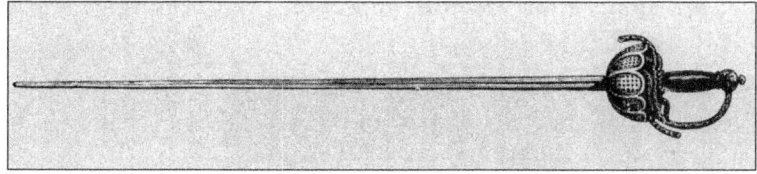

Sixteenth century rapier.

During the early part of the fourteenth century the German masters of arms formed an association called *Burgerschaft von St Marcus von Lowenberg* (*The Citizens of St. Marcus of Lowenberg*). It was the work of this association which put them at the forefront of practical fencing application. In fact, research shows that Hans Lebkommer (1535) was perhaps responsible for the first authoritative book on this art form: *Der Alten Fechter Grundliche Kunst* (*Complete Teachings of the Old Fencers*). Therefore, it can reasonably be assumed that prior to the mid-sixteenth century, the German was among the most proficient in the use of the two-handed sword and the sword and buckler (curved shield), the preferred weapons of the time. Although the German exponent of fence was adept at sword play, the sword practitioners from Italy were actually responsible for systematizing this fighting form. The

Bolognese fencing master, Achille Marozzo, wrote his now-famous work on the art, *Opera Nova*, in 1536. This book describes the characteristics of sword play during Europe's fifteenth and sixteenth centuries. It was throughout these centuries that appreciation for the effectiveness of the sword-point for thrusting was again rediscovered (Nadi, 1943). The *estoc* (span.), a precursor to the rapier, was the weapon which revolutionized this rediscovery. In fact, the attributes of this sword's application laid the foundation of the Philippine fencing form known as *estokada* (span., imperfectly acquired, assimilated into Tagalog language). The estoc's design is long, flexible, and pointed, making it an excellent weapon for penetrating small openings in armor. Furthermore, with the decline in the use of full-body armor, heavy cutting and hacking swords were no longer in vogue as the lighter and more versatile estoc and rapier proved adequate.

The fencing style of Marozzo was rooted in the implementation of the double-edged sword, a weapon with which he utilized cutting maneuvers from either edge of the blade—an obvious advantage to its employer. According to Arthur Wise (1971), the techniques in Marozzo's system consisted of the *mandritti* (cuts against an opponent's left side) and the rovers (cuts against an opponent's right side) and blows classified according to their direction of execution such as the *tondo* (horizontal slash), *montante* (vertical slash), *fendente* (upward or downward slash), and the *squalambrato* (oblique slash). These stroking classifications are similar to those found in many classical eskrima systems of the Philippines.

Whereas Marozzo concentrated on the use of the rapier as an instrument of cutting, Camillo Agrippa can be regarded as the man responsible for introducing its use as an instrument of thrusting. The rapier, although including any number of hilt designs, is long and tapers to a diamond-shape point, not unlike the Philippine *yantòk* (tag., tapered fighting stick). Agrippa's disciple, Giacomo di Grassi, published a book in 1594 entitled *His True Arte of Defence*. He regarded the techniques of thrusting more efficient than those of slashing. He developed a cutting and thrusting rapier with a basket hilt called the "single sword." Grassi was also responsible for defining four areas, or angles, of attack—a concept which is of paramount importance to the study of classical eskrima.

It was Grassi who popularized the use of the dagger as the ultimate defensive tool when employed as a supplement to the rapier in combat. This was revolutionary for until that time the buckler was in standard use. Grassi, therefore, can be thought of as the father of the "rapier and dagger" fencing style which later became popularly known in the Philippines as *"espada y daga"* (span., sword and dagger).

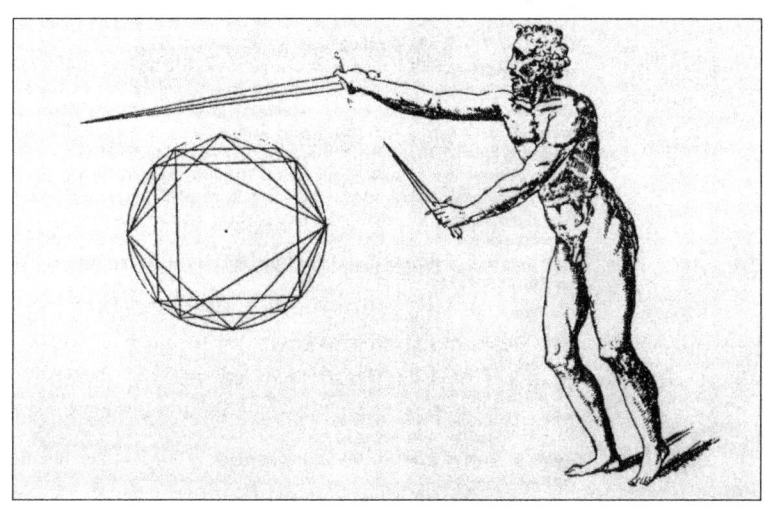

Angles of attack rendered according
to Camillo Agrippa's description.
*Illustration by Carlos R. Aldrete.*

The use of a "case of rapiers" (i.e., two-sword fencing) had also come into play during the European Renaissance. Although many presumed that the use of two equally measured weapons would be somewhat cumbersome in combat (hence proving ineffective), many masters encouraged their students to develop this skill. It was believed that by practicing with two weapons of equal length (one in each hand) the fencing student would develop ambidexterity. This attribute would afford him the ability to switch hands and remain effective in combat, should his offensive hand or arm be severely wounded. The use of the so-called "case of rapiers" is a precursor to the *doble baston* (span., double sticks; imperfectly acquired and assimilated into Tagalog language) system of classical eskrima.

Although influence of the Italian fencing movement was felt throughout Europe, it seemed to have had little effect on those systems of Spanish origin. The Spanish swordsman was a person of great fencing skill and knowledge who developed a system of sword play which was a force to be reckoned with. This Spanish fencing system developed outside of the mainstream of European swordsmanship as evidenced by its relative separation and isolation from evolving schools in Italy, Germany, and England. The very fact that it survived into the eighteenth century is testament to its effectiveness.

Jeronimo de Carranza and Luis Pacheco y Narvaez are two fencing masters whose names dominated Spanish fencing circles during the eighteenth century. In fact, appreciation for their efforts has endured well into this century. In 1582, Carranza published his definitive text on sword play, *Libro Que Tratta ella Philosophia de las Armas* (*Book on the Philosophy of Arms*). Narvaez (1600), Carranza's disciple, published his text entitled *Libro de las Grandezas de la Espada* (*Book on the Greatness of the Sword*). Carranza and Narvaez were known to have possessed a great deal of knowledge in the areas of mathematics and philosophy. Interestingly, the most distinctive quality of Spanish sword play theory is its deep intellectual and philosophical roots. Perhaps the greatest virtue of the Spanish master of fence was his ability to maintain a calm state of mind, which afforded him accurate calculation when engaged in a duel. Apparently, these calculations were not accurate enough for the late Ferdinand Magellan, however, as evidenced by his poor judgment in engaging Raja Lapu Lapu and his warriors on Mactan Island on April 27, 1521.

**The Spanish Influence on Kali**

The Spanish method of wielding European swords was transplanted to the Philippines in 1521 with the voyage of Ferdinand Magellan. Magellan, sailing under the flag of Spain, was in search of a westward route across the Pacific. Magellan was never to complete the first circumnavigation of the world as he was killed in the infamous battle of Mactan. The historian, Antonio Pigafeta, who chronicled Magellan's voyage, wrote a rather detailed account of this battle in his text, *Magellan's Voyage*, for those who are interested in the finer details (see Pigafeta, 1969). In terms of presenting the history of the Filipino martial arts, this account is somewhat superficial. I will, however, offer a brief summary.

On Saturday, March 27, 1521, Ferdinand Magellan's ship came across an archipelago which was, until then, unknown to the Western world. He docked off the coast of Zamal (Samar) Island. On March 18, he became acquainted with Raja Kolambu, the chief of Zamal, as well as Raja Humabon, the chief of Zugbu (Cebu). He converted them to Catholicism and a short-lived Spanish allegiance. In a counter-intelligence ploy by Humabon, Magellan agreed to attack Mactan Island, conquer it, and offer it as a token gift of friendship to Humabon. Armed with their *kampilan* (tag., cutlass; long, straight sabre broadening toward the point), *sibat* (tag., spears), *sinugba sa apòy* (tag., [sticks] hardened in fire), and *kalasag* (tag., shield), Lapu Lapu's warriors repelled these invaders, killing Magellan in the low tide that forced him into a hand-to-hand skirmish rather than a ship-based bombardment of the island. According to Gonzales (1800), *pangamut*, the kali system of Raja Lapu Lapu, consisted of six slashes (to the head, chest and kidneys, both left and right sides) and two thrusts (to the face and abdominal region).

In 1564, the Spanish gained a foothold in the Philippines through the efforts of Miguel Lopez de Legaspi. Legaspi, remembering the plight of Magellan, befriended the natives he encountered and later "conquered" them by gaining their trust and converting them to the Catholic faith. He was responsible for the first Spanish settlement and colonial government in Manila in 1571 and was consequently honored by Raja Malitik by being given a demonstration of *kali* and *buno* (Yambao, 1957).

After a number of skirmishes against the *katutubong mandirigma Pilipino* (tag., native Filipino warriors), who were opposed to Spanish rule, under the decree of King Phillip II of Spain, the Spanish Royal Audencia was established in Manila to suppress the practice of kali. In 1597, the Spanish forced the abandonment of the sultanate in Manila, which had been established in 1565. Hence, the presence of the *komedya* stage plays. The *komedya* were socio-religious plays depicting the victory of the Christian Spaniards over the Muslim Moors of Africa. It was used as propaganda by the Spanish friars to spread Catholicism throughout the Philippine Archipelago by showing the superiority of the Christian faith over the natives' paganistic beliefs. In time, more plays emerged for the Spaniards' enjoyment. These plays were viewed by the Filipino as a way to practice their warrior arts under the guise of harmless entertainment.

In 1610, *arnes de mano* (span., harness of the hands), became the new name used by the Spanish on Luzon to describe the movements of the ornamental hand trappings decorating the Filipino actors' costumes. The term eskrima was coined by the Spaniards in the Visayan Island region after witnessing a fight between two Filipino stick fighters. The terms are somewhat interchangeable—although some would disagree—as they represent a single martial art form which was developed under repressive circumstances over a specific period of time. Although many people of the Philippines complied with Spanish rule, many natives continued to feel repressed. This repression led to a number of Filipino rebellions, such as the Rebellion of Diego Silang (1762-1763), the Palaris Revolt (1762-1765), and the Cagayan Uprising (1763). In 1764, Don Simon de Anda y Salazar prohibited the brandishing of the dagger and *bolo* (tag., eighteen inch long knife; machete) (Yambao, 1957). He did this in order to prevent future revolts by denying the Filipinos access to bladed weapons. From then on, eskrima was practiced with long and short sticks (Lañada and Mariñas, 1974).

Prior to the Philippine Revolution of 1896, a man named Don Jose de Azes operated a school of Spanish fencing and Filipino eskrima. The school was called *Tanghalan ng Sandata* (tag., Gallery of Weapons), and was located inside the *Ateneo de Manila* (span.), an exclusive Jesuit high school where the upper-class teenagers of Manila studied (Karnow, 1989). Tanghalan ng Sandata was a place where many future leaders of the Philippine Revolution met and practiced eskrima (Yambao, 1957). The Filipino national hero Jose Rizal y Mercado was a graduate of the Ateneo de Manila. Rizal eventual went on to study medicine, philosophy, literature, several languages, and arts and crafts and to practice fencing at the University of Madrid where he later rallied against Spanish oppression in the Philippines. Rizal, with the editorial help of Marcelo H. del Pilar, formed a Filipino movement called the Propagandists. They published (in addition to a number of brochures and pamphlets) a newspaper called *La Solidaridad* (span., *The Solidarity*), a vehicle by which they publicly opposed Spanish political, economic and social policies in the Philippines. One of Rizal's contemporaries, Juan Luna, also studied in Europe and became a fencing expert, in addition to his mastery of eskrima. Luna was also a distinguished painter, who, along with Felix Resurrecion, won high honors in a contest for Spanish artists. His brother, Antonio Luna, on the other hand, became a great military leader during the Philippine Revolution. He, too, was an accomplished practitioner of escrima (Karnow, 1989).

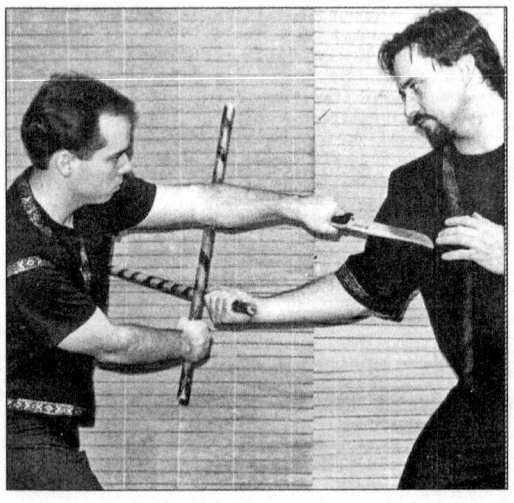

Mark V. Wiley, practicing with espada y daga.
*Photo by Carlos R. Aldrete.*

Through repression and rebellion, the ancient Philippine art of kali was altered. This coupled with the tremendous influence of Spanish culture prompted the evolution of eskrima, the classical fighting art of the Filipino. It was indeed the Spanish rapier and dagger systems which had the greatest influence on the evolution of eskrima from kali. The use of numbered angles of attack and what have become the traditional eskrima uniforms were products of the transplanted and assimilated Spanish culture. It is also interesting that although Filipino (a Tagalog-based language) is now the national language of the Philippines, many *eskrimadors* (tag.; derived from *esgrimadores*, span., those who fence) use Spanish as the language in which they teach their martial arts.

Venancio "Ansiong" Bacon, founder of the Balintawak style.
*Photo courtesy of Bakbakan International.*

## On Classical Eskrima

The classical arts of eskrima are characterized by their nearly exclusive use of weaponry. Their techniques are those kali movements which changed over time through the strong influence of Spanish fencing forms. In fact, it would be hard to distinguish some systems of eskrima from their Spanish counterparts if it weren't for the obvious preference for blunt sticks over fencing foils, epees, and sabres.

There are many similarities between the stages of learning the arts of fencing and eskrima. Castello and Castello (1962) refer to four stages of fencing practice: (1) understanding the progression of learning and the fundamentals, (2) practice drills, (3) practice bouts, and (4) competitive bouts. Yambao (1957) divides the training of eskrima (arnis) into four stages: (1) *muestracion* (span., demonstration), (2) *sangga at patama* (tag.; e.g., give- and-take drills), (3) *labanangmalapitan* (tag., close-quarter combat), and (4) *labanang malayuan* (tag., long-range fighting). These stages prepare the eskrimador for *labanang tutu-hanan* (tag., actual combat).

The characteristics most associated with classical eskrima are different from those characteristics found in various ancient kali systems (which display characteristics of Indo-Malayan silat), or the many modern eskrima and arnis systems (which include various elements of the Japanese/Okinawan styles). These include techniques of *dobleng* (tag., double; e.g., circular stroking patterns), *lastiko* (tag., elastic; e.g., the forward and backward leaning of the body), and the back-held position of the "alive hand" (tag., *bantay-kamay*). Classical eskrima is generally described as developing combat skills in the primary areas of the single stick (solo baston, span., imperfectly assimilated into Tagalog language), double sticks, stick and dagger (*baston y daga*, span., imperfectly assimilated into Tagalog language), and sword and dagger. Marinas (1988) notes that by the early seventeenth century the metallic sword was replaced by a long stick. Thus, the term "espada y daga" refers to the practice of stick and dagger and/or long-and-short-stick eskrima training. In recent history many masters of the classical systems, such as Herminia B. Biñas, Sr. have added the dimension of hand-to-hand combat (*mano-mano*, span., imperfectly assimilated into Tagalog language) and bayonet defenses to their repertoire. These developmental changes emerged as Biñas was actively involved in instructing the Philippine armed forces during World War II. This evolution began the "modern era" of eskrima and arnis in the Philippines, as seen today in modern tournament competitions.

1) Angel Cabales, founder of Cabalas Serrada Escrima. 2) Amante Mariñas of Pananandata. 3) Antonio Ilustrisimo, founder of Kali Ilustrisimo. 4) Jose Caballero of de Campo Uno-Dos-Tres Original. 5) Timoteo Maranga of Tres Personas Arnis. *Photos 3, 4, and 5 courtesy of Bakbakan International. Photo 2 courtesy of A. Manilas. Photo 1 by Alan McLuckie.*

Placido Yambao, with the editorial assistance of Buenaventura Mirafuente, wrote the first book on the Filipino martial arts. Their text, entitled

*Mga Karunungan sa Larung Arnis* (*Knowledge in the Art of Arnis*), was published in 1957. In 1974, Porferio S. Lañada and Amante P. Mariñas wrote the first English text on a Filipino martial art. It was entitled *Arnis De Mano*. Benjamin Luna Lema is one of the few others to publish a work on the classical Filipino martial art. In 1989, he published *Arnis: Filipino Art of Stick Fighting*, a now out-of-print text on his so-called Lightning Scientific Arnis System. Edgar G. Sulite's texts, *The Secrets of Arnis* (1986) and *Advanced Balisong* (1987), and Dan Inosanto and Gilbert Johnson's text, *The Filipino Martial Arts* (1980), have also described elements of the ancient kali systems. Conversely, Ciriaco Cañete's book, *Doce Pares: Basic Arnis, Eskrima, Pangolisi* (1988), as well as Grandmaster Remy Presas' *Modern Arnis: Filipino Art of Stick Fighting* (1983), are two works concerned with the modern eskrima/arnis systems.

Left: Carlito A. Lañada, of Kuntaw Lima-Lima. *Photo by Carlos Aldrete.*
Right: Herminia B. Berminia B. Biñas, Sr., founder of Biñas Dynamic
Arnis, instructing M. Wiley. *Photo by David Smith.*

## Further Analysis

There are as many systems or styles of Filipino martial arts as there are islands in the Philippines and practitioners living on them. Although the various arts certainly have a number of similarities in their respective training methods and physical application, they can be generally classified into eight categories: provincial styles (e.g., Bicolano arnis; Pangasinan eskrima); personal styles (e.g., Bifias dynamic arnis; kali Ilustrisimo); styles defined by technical characteristic (e.g., abaniko style; sinawali style), or fighting range (e.g., serrada escrima; larga mano arnis); styles consisting of composite systems (e.g., Vee arnis-jitsu; lameco eskrima); eclectic styles (e.g., talahib fighting arts); empty-hand systems (e.g., sagasa kickboxing; hagibis combat system), and those styles named after their enemies (e.g., Etalanio style).

The classical arts of eskrima are becoming exceedingly rare today as many masters prefer to utilize the Japanese trappings of colored-belt ranking, the karate *gi* (japan., uniform), and various throws and break-falling techniques "borrowed" from such Japanese martial arts as aikido, judo, and jujutsu. This evolution can be seen in the modern escrido system developed by Ciriaco Cañete of the famed Doce Pares Club (founded in 1932) and the Modern Arnis system of Remy Presas. These recent developments have led to the next generation or "modern era" of the Filipino martial arts. Although these recent changes are not necessarily wrong and constitute a natural evolution of the art, classical eskrima, the Filipino fencing form, may soon be little more than a memory like its ancient counterpart, kali.

### Languages
| | |
|---|---|
| Arabic | arb. |
| Chinese | chin. |
| Indonesian | indo |
| Japanese | japan. |
| Pangasinan | pang. |
| Sanskrit | skt. |
| Spanish | span. |
| Taglog | tag. |
| Visayan | vis. |

### Notes

[1] Yambao (1957) equates the shortened term *kali* as having derived from such terms as *pagkalikali* (ibanag), *kalirongan* (pang.), *kaliradman* (vis.). Presas (1983) posits that the art derived from the Indonesian fencing form of *tjakalele*. Maliszewski (1992) notes several possible derivations such as from the name of the black and bloody Hindu goddess Kali, consort of the Hindu god Siva, as well as a possible derivation from Visayan word roots: *ka-kamut* (hand) and *li-lihok* (movement). Others claim that an art called *silak* was the original fighting art in the Philippines and that the term *kalis*, from which *kali* derives, comes from the reverse spelling of *silak* (Christopher Sayoc, personal communication, March, 1992). Still others equate the term with an abbreviation of *Kalimantan* (Borneo), the island from which the ten datus fled, eventually establishing the bothoan on Panay, Philippines.

[2] Sulaiman Sharif (personal communication, July, 1991), believes that the

art of kali is based on the foundations and footwork (i.e., *langka*) of silat. Fernando Amilbangsa (1983) likens *langka* to a martial dance identified with male performers. "The square line direction of movement, the postures and the gestures closely resemble those of certain Asian martial arts forms, particularly of Malaysia and Indonesia" (p. 14).

3 Although the Spaniards are credited with "discovering" the Philippines, the archipelago were previously visited by Asian pygmies (25,000-30,000 years ago), the Indonesians (from 3,000 to 500 B.C.E.), the Malaysians (from 300 B.C.E. to 1600 C.E.), followed by visits from India (seventh century), China (ninth century), and Arabia (fifteenth century). As noted by Zaide (1979, p. 381), the Portuguese, although not often acknowledged for doing so, visited the Philippines almost a decade before Magellan:

> In 1512, while exploring the waters off Moluccas, Francisco Serrano was shipwrecked, and took refuge at the coast of Mindanao [A]nother Portuguese, Duarte Barbosa ... wrote of Sulu in 1516, implying Portuguese knowledge of that island in the Philippines. Archival records in Lisbon indicate that Portuguese ships from the Moluccas frequented the waters of southern Philippines from 1512 to 1565.

4 Once known as *baybayin* and *abakada* and commonly referred to as *alibata*, the ancient Philippine alphabet is believed to have been brought to the archipelago by the Tamil of Malaya about 200 B.C.E. (Francisco, 1980).

5 The *Maragtas*, written in 1250 by Datu Sumakwel, is the written history of Panay. Although many have written about this book and its contents, as Francisco (1980) and Zaide (1979) have noted, it is conspicuous by its absence. Therefore, any research based on its content should be considered speculative.

6 Ben Largusa (personal communication, June, 1993) believes that the arts of kali and silat are, for all intent and purposes, identical.

7 Islam was brought to the Philippines in 1450 by Abu Bakr, a Bornean trader. After successfully uniting the islands of the Sulu Archipelago, he established himself as *Sultan* (arb., highest religious and political authority) (Spencer, 1993).

8 *Katipunan* is the accepted abbreviation for *Kataastaasang Kagalanggalang katipunan ng mga Anak ng Bayan* (tag., The Exalted and Most Honorable Society of the Sons of the People). Formed in 1892 by Andres Bonifacio, the *katipunan* was a nineteenth century Philippine independence movement which opposed Spain's governing policies in the Philippines.

9 *The Art and History of Personal Combat* (Wise, 1970) is a good general

reference book on the evolution of hand-to-hand combat in Europe throughout the centuries. The author, however, was somewhat lax in his citation of sources as evidenced by the often misspelled book titles, authors' names, and incorrect publication dates found within the body of the work.

## References

Canete, C. (1988). *Doce pares: Basic eskrima, arnis, Pangolisi*. Cebu, Philippines: Doce Pares Publishing House.

Canete, D. A. (1993). *The Philippines eskrima, kali, arnis*. Cebu, Philippines: Doce Pares Publishing House.

Castello, H., and Castello, J. (1962). *Fencing*. New York: The Roland Press.

Draeger, D. F. (1979). *Weapons and fighting arts of the Indonesian archipelago*. Tokyo: Charles E. Tuttle.

Draeger, D. F., and Chambers, Q. (1978). *Javanese silat: The fighting art of perisai diri*. Tokyo: Kodansha International.

Draeger, D. F., and Smith, R. W. (1980). *Comprehensive Asian fighting arts*. Tokyo: Kodansha International.

Fernando-Amilbangsa, L. (1983). *Pangalay*. Manila, Philippines: Filipinas Foundation.

Francisco, J. R. (1980, March). Tracing the origin of the Philippine syllabary. *Archipelago: The international magazine of the Philippines*. pp. 11-14.

Frey, E. (1986). *The kris: Mystic weapon of the Malay world*. New York: Oxford University.

Gonzales, D. B. (1800). *De los delitos* [Of the crimes]. Madrid, Spain.

Hamzuri, Drs. (1984). Keris (J. Achjadi, Trans.). Jakarta, Indonesia: Djambatan.

Inosanto, D., and Johnson, G. (1980). *The Filipino martial arts*. Los Angeles: Know Now.

Karnow, S. (1989). *In our image: America's empire in the Philippines*. New York: Random House.

Kessler, R. J. (1989). *Rebellion and repression in the Philippines*. New Haven, CT: Yale University.

Lañada, P. S., and Mariñas, A. P. (1974). *Arnis de mano*. Elmhurst, NY: Arnis de Mano.

Lema, B. L. (1989). *Arnis: Filipino art of self defense*. Metro Manila, Philippines: Integrated Publishing House.

Maliszewski, M. (1992a). Medical, healing and spiritual components of Asian martial arts. *Journal of Asian Martial Arts, 1*(2), 24-57.

Maliszewski, M. (1992b). Meditative-religious traditions of fighting arts and martial ways. *Journal of Asian Martial Arts, 1*(3), 30-32, 55.

Marinas, A. P. (1986). *Pananandata knife fighting*. Boulder, CO: Paladin.

Marinas, A. P. (1988). *Pananandata yantok at daga*. Boulder, CO: Paladin.

McKay, J. P., Hill, B. D., and Buckler, J. (1991). *A history of western society*. Boston: Houghton Mifflin Company.

Nadi, A. (1943). *On fencing*. New York: G. P. Putnam's Sons.

Pigafetta, A. (1969). *Magellan's voyage: A narrative account of the first circumnavigation*. New Haven, CT: Yale University.

Presas, E. A. (1988). *Arnis: Presas style and balisong*. Manila, Philippines: Ernesto Presas.

Presas, R. (1983). *Modern arnis: Filipino art of stick fighting*. Burbank: O'Hara.

Scott, W. H. (1984). *Prehispanic source material for the study of Philippine history*. Quezon City: New Day.

Sinnigen, W., and Boak, A. (1977). *A history of Rome to A.D. 565*. New York: MacMillan.

Solyom, G., and Solyom, B. (1978). *The world of the Javanese keris*. Honolulu, Hawaii: Asian Arts Press.

Spencer, A. M. (1993). *Island mosiac: The arts of the Philippines*. Newark, New Jersey: The Newark Museum.

St. Clair, F. (1991). *The katipunan*. Metro Manila, Philippines: Solar.

Sulite, E. G. (1986). *The secrets of arnis*. San Juan, Philippines: Socorro.

Sulite, E. G. (1987). *Advanced balisong*. San Juan, Philippines: Socorro.

Tiongson, N. G. (ed.). (1991). *Tuklas sining*. Manila: Cultural Center of the Philippines.

Tudisco, A. J. (1966). *Asia emerges*. Berkeley, CA: Diablo.

Wiley, M. V. (1992a, September). The crippling kicks of escrima. *Black Belt*, pp. 34-37.

Wiley, M. V. (1992b, March/April). Herminio Biñas and the art of arnis. *Eskrima Review*, pp. 2-5.

Wiley, M. V. (1994). *Filipino Martial Arts: Cabales serrada escrima*. Tokyo: Charles E. Tuttle.

Wise, A. (1971). *The art and history of personal combat*. Greenwich, CT: Arma Press.

Yambao, P. (1957). *Mga karunungan sa larung arnis* [Knowledge in the art of arnis] (M. Buenaventura, Ed.) (R. S. Galang, Trans.). Quezon City, Philippines: University of the Philippines.

Zaide, G. F. (1979). *The pageant of Philippine history*. Manila: Philippine Education Company.

chapter 2

# The Classification and Ethos of Filipino Martial Traditions

by Mark V. Wiley, B.S.

Left: Oonfre C. Escorpizo, master of the Pangasinan style of Cinco Tero Eskrima. Right: Ramiro U. Estalilla, grandmaster of the Rigonan-Estalilla system of Kabaroan, posing here in traditional Fraile-style uniform with kampilan sword. *All photographs courtesy of M. Wiley except where noted.*

Researchers investigating martial culture in India, China, and Japan usually analyze family-owned manuscripts (India), classical texts (China), and *kadensho* transmission-scrolls (Japan) to determine the nature and evolution of various martial practices and techniques. This is a task requiring many years work even if confined to specific texts or particular time periods in history. Unfortunately, as the martial arts later spread into Southeast Asia, the use of such documents disappeared. It is unclear as to why this was the case. One may speculate that this may have had something to do with the destruction that resulted from the many invasions in this area (e.g., the Spanish invasion of the Philippines and the subsequent destruction and burning of records, writings, and other artifacts).

As a result of these occurrences, researchers attempting to explore Filipino martial culture are often frustrated by the lack of documentation to support their investigations. Moreover, the books that practitioners have written are often simply transcribed oral history. Much of the information contained in such books is indicative of the characteristic weaknesses of oral historiography:

1) historical dates are often inaccurate; 2) legends are taken at face value; 3) exaggerated claims are made concerning an individual's martial prowess; and 4) the heroic feats of culture heroes are taken as fact and recorded in the written word as if they were true. Conversely, through the transmission of oral history one can learn many things: 1) intimate details about a master's life-history; 2) "rites of passage" involved in martial arts training; and 3) the actual events surrounding challenge matches in contemporary Filipino society, thus dispelling the perpetuation of recent myths.

For these reasons, oral historiography is considered a legitimate method of inquiry in researching various aspects of Filipino culture today (see Foronda, 1981). Demetrio's (1978: 65) position on this is well taken: ". . . oral tradition is concerned not with authorship or the fact. . . . Most of the time what is handed down as tradition has no author, nor can it be fully established as 'fact' always. Yet the fact that a story, a proverb, a myth is handed down either orally or in writing, whether in its entirety or in part, argues for its value and importance for both the tradition bearers and receivers."

To illustrate this point further, one may consider the myth associated with Lapulapu regarding the origin of Filipino martial arts. To consider this creation myth in general, one must consider the position taken by most martial arts practitioners in tracing the origins of their systems. To begin with, many practitioners of East Asian martial arts purport to trace the origins of their systems back to Bodhidharma, despite high quality scholarship indicating otherwise (Faure, 1986; Maliszewski, 1992). Related more specifically to a single system of martial arts, many practitioners of taijiquan identify its originator as Zhang Sanfeng (Chang San-feng), again despite evidence to the contrary (Hu, 1964; Wong, 1979). A similar parallel is found in the Filipino martial arts tradition with attempts of Christianized Filipino masters to trace the lineage of their respective martial systems to Lapulapu. This is particularly interesting in that Lapulapu was from Mactan Island (Visayas, central Philippines) and many of these masters are from Manila (Luzon, northern Philippines). In addition, Lapulapu became the first national hero of the Philippines for repelling the Spanish conquistadores, whose religion and language these masters currently embrace. While the connection between Lapulapu and these masters' respective martial arts is historically and geographically unfounded, their belief in this connection is still important. Anthropologically speaking, the historical accuracy of these accounts is less important than what these practitioners say and why they say it. It is precisely these creation myths that provide the martial arts practitioner with a sense of meaning, identity, and orientation to world historical events in general. To this end, Rosaldo (1986: 98) suggests that the researcher ". . . can learn much about meaningful action by listening to storytellers as they depict their own lives."

For the reasons noted above, the purpose of my research has been to classify Filipino martial arts and explore the ethos of Filipino martial culture by deriving information directly from the contemporary grandmasters who have maintained an oral transmission of information concerning the evolution and development of their respective martial systems. I have also relied upon primary and secondary written sources and 18 years of participant observation.

## Classification of Filipino Martial Arts

A common misconception with respect to Filipino martial arts is that there is only one indigenous martial art in the Philippines (i.e., kali). Many contemporary instructors and writers assert that the respective terms for the martial arts of kali, eskrima, and arnis (among a shopping list of others) are synonymous and represent one single martial art form (see, for example, Sulite, 1986; Yambao, 1957). This problem is confounded by the fact that instructors of the various arts tend to change the names of their systems from arnis to kali to eskrima, for example, whenever one term becomes more popular than another. Others claim that the latter two arts are but mere "phases" of kali, the so-called "mother art" of the Philippines (Inosanto, 1977). Contrary to common beliefs, current research findings (see Wiley, in press-b) indicate that there are perhaps over 200 martial arts "systems" in the Philippines, and an even greater number of collateral Filipino "sub-systems" and personalized "styles" currently practiced around the world.

Since Indonesian pencak-silat and Malaysian langka-silat predate Filipino kali as martial arts in the Philippines, one naturally concludes that kali cannot be the "mother art" of the Philippines as so many writers suggest. Are we to assume that the hypothesis classifying eskrima and arnis as "phases" of kali is sound just because they evolved from the latter art? If so, would it not follow, then, that the art of kali is but a "phase" of silat, its precursor? If this classification is to be used, then it would also follow that silat is at once the "mother art" and the only "complete" martial art in the Philippines. Such a contention is both naive and absurd.

This classification theory is further refuted when one considers the vast number of native grappling arts that survive to this day among various indigenous tribal and ethnic groups in the Philippines. Tribes such as the Ifugao, Samal, Igorot, Ibanag, Manobo, Dumagat, and Maranaw practice grappling arts known as *bultong, silaga, dama, garong, buteng, purgos,* and *kapulubod*.

Various ethnic groups such as the Tagalog, Ilokano, Cebuano, Bicolano, Pampanga, Pangasinan, and Panayeno practice grappling arts known as *gabbo*, *layung*, *lampugan*, *pantok*, *balsakan*, and *dumog* (Anima, 1982). Any attempt to label these indigenous grappling arts as one and the same based on their shared unarmed, grappling characteristics would do much to deny the Filipino his inherited right of autonomous tribal/ethnic expression. In addition, these grappling arts were practiced in the Philippines prior to the spread of the Indonesian and Malaysian silat systems. Therefore, they cannot be a "phase" of kali—an art grounded in the techniques of silat and structured around the use of bladed weapons.

The theory of a single indigenous Filipino martial art is further disproven in its apparent dismissal of the practice of martial arts transplanted and maintained in whole from other Asian countries (e.g., the practice of Chinese kuntao and Indonesian and Malaysian silat systems by the Samal and Tausug tribes of the southern Philippines). Furthermore, the contemporary empty hand systems of *sikaran*, *yaw-yan*, *sagasa*, and *hagibis*, for example, belong to neither the weapons-based systems of kali, eskrima, or arnis nor are they related to kuntao or silat. It is not possible, then, for these arts to be classified as a "phase" of kali (or silat).

As is indicated by the results of this study (see appendix), it is clear that the martial arts of contemporary Filipino grandmasters tend to fall into one of three classifications: "ancient," "classical," or "modern." (For a detailed description of what comprises these classifications and how they were constructed, see the appendix). The martial arts found in the twentieth century Philippines are the culmination of an evolutionary process that includes influences from central Asia, India, Malaysia, Indonesia, China, Europe, the United States, and Japan. It is therefore impossible to define the "classical" systems of eskrima or the "modern" systems of arnis as "phases" of any art that did not evolve during their respective time-periods.

The "classical" art of eskrima evolved during a three-century ban (1565-1898) on the "ancient" martial art of kali. Therefore, its curriculum encompasses many elements of European swordplay that the preserved "ancient" arts do not. Initially, eskrima was practiced with long and short sticks—even the brandishing of the general utility bolo was prohibited. Since Western fencing became a favorite past time among *mestizos* (Filipinos of Spanish descent), sticks were later replaced by European-style edged weapons such as the *estoc*. The footwork patterns of the "classical" systems tend to be structured around a triangle set between two parallel lines. Moreover, while eskrima systems tend to have an elaborate repertoire of hand-to-weapon defenses, they have only marginal hand-to-hand fighting techniques.

As a result of Philippine independence from Spain and subsequent cultural contacts with the United States and Japan (1898–present), a number of contemporary Filipino masters have developed "modern" martial arts such as arnis, sikaran, and hagibis. These "modern" martial arts generally feature the inclusion of hand-to-hand defensive techniques largely incorporated from any combination of Okinawan karate; Japanese karate, aikido, and judo; Korean taekwondo; and Chinese wushu sources. Moreover, they tend to lack sophisticated footwork with training essentially centered around modern sport competition.

Generally speaking, the "ancient" arts of kali are structured around the use of Indonesian and Malaysian swords (i.e., *kris, barong, kampilan*), the use of indigenous projectile weapons (i.e., *sumpit* [blow gun], *pana* [bow and arrow]), the use of flexible weapons (i.e., *tanikala* [chain], *panyo* [handkerchief]), with footwork patterns structured around elaborate geometric shapes. Preserved in the unconquered Muslim areas of the southern Philippines, kali did not undergo the same evolutionary process as did eskrima and arnis. Therefore, the "ancient" art of kali could not possibly have maintained eskrima or arnis in its curricular content—Spain, the United States, and Japan had not yet, at the height of this art's popularity in the archipelago (prehistory-C.E. 1521), dominated the Philippines.

Theoretically speaking, there are as many "styles" of Filipino martial arts as there are practitioners living in the Philippines. It is the close connection between these islands and their martial inhabitants that embodies the whole of Filipino martial arts as a subculture of the larger, encompassing Philippine Island identity. Martial arts show great variety in the Philippines. Indeed, even within a given region there is variation in martial practices. On the northern island of Luzon, for example, one can find weapon systems referred to as *kadaanan*, meaning "ancient" or "of the old," which embrace angular footwork and close range tactics; systems referred to as *kabaroan*, meaning "modern" or "of the new," which embrace linear footwork and long range tactics; stick-fighting systems known as *cinco tero*, which revolve solely around the use of five strikes; and various indigenous wrestling systems among the Igorot cultures. Such differences can be found within every major region of the Philippines. This variation is due primarily to the isolation of regional populations, which in times past hindered diffusion of the arts. In addition, the desire of various practitioners of the arts to become respected as founders of systems have led many masters to introduce new innovations which resulted in a number of collateral systems from a common root art. This process has contributed to a variety of systematic and technical differences among and between Filipino martial arts in the three primary island regions (Luzon, the Visayas, and Mindanao).

Conversely, as a result of continuous cultural contact between Philippine tribal and ethnic groups over the past fifty years and the subsequent invasions of the archipelago by foreign powers, one certainly finds various martial arts in contemporary Philippines embracing common training methods and martial applications. In fact, a closer investigation into these systems' founding locations, martial techniques, and subsequent naming determines that Filipino martial arts generally can be grouped into nine categories: 1) provincial styles (e.g., Bicolano arnis; arnis Pangasinan); 2) personal styles (e.g., Biñas dynamic arnis; kali Ilustrisimo); 3) styles defined by technical characteristic (e.g., lapunti arnis de abaniko; doblete rapillon); 4) fighting range (e.g., Cabales serrada escrima; lameco eskrima); 5) systems consisting of composite styles (e.g., Vee arnis-jitsu); 6) empty hand systems (e.g., sagasa; hagibis); 7) styles named after historic places (e.g., Balintawak eskrima) and 8) national heroes (e.g, Lapulapu kali; tabak ni Bonifacio); and 9) styles named after the weapons of former enemies (e.g., *espada y daga; estoque*).

One may suspect that every martial art that has survived the plague of time is effective in combat. This is not necessarily so. A number of martial arts, Filipino and otherwise, have maintained their status through tradition although their techniques have largely become antiquated. A number of other systems are contemporary creations and have yet to be proven in an actual confrontation. Thus, many martial arts are more theoretical than practical.

Contemporary grandmasters of the Filipino martial arts unanimously assert that their respective systems are the most effective in the world. In addition, many claim to be undefeated in "death-matches," which, of course, leads one to believe that they never fought one another in such contests. It is not possible that every master possesses the most effective techniques. If this were the case, then a form of martial Darwinism would have taken place, leaving only the most effective martial art to exist in contemporary society. What we find in the Philippines and the United States, rather, is quite a diverse array of Filipino martial arts. Each of these systems and their derivative styles are certainly more effective in certain areas than in others. Thus, many martial arts flourish, each effective in its own right. Moreover, these systems are better suited to certain individuals than to others, based on their general movement characteristics. In this way, the personalities of the masters have contributed greatly to the diversity of the Filipino martial arts. The presence of so many ethnic groups in the Philippines further adds to the uniqueness of its martial arts masters and the diversity, structure, and characteristic of their martial arts systems. Thus, there appears to be no simple blending, no unified art, no unified philosophy, but nine categories of martial arts (as noted above) corresponding to the three classifications of "ancient," "classical," and "modern." Given these observations, it is now appropriate to examine the ethos of Filipino martial culture in relation to that of other Asian countries.

## Technique of the "Ancient" Martial Art of Kali Ilustrisimo
### Empty-Hand vs. Knife Attack

Master Tony Diego (right) prepares to defend against a knife attack initiated by Master Christopher Ricketts (fig. 1). As the knife nears, Diego steps to the left while parrying the attacking arm and thrusting to the eyes of the attacker (fig. 2). Since the thrust was deflected, the attacker attempts a second, higher thrust that is also blocked (fig. 3). Diego then executes a wrist lock and begins to disarm the knife (fig. 4).

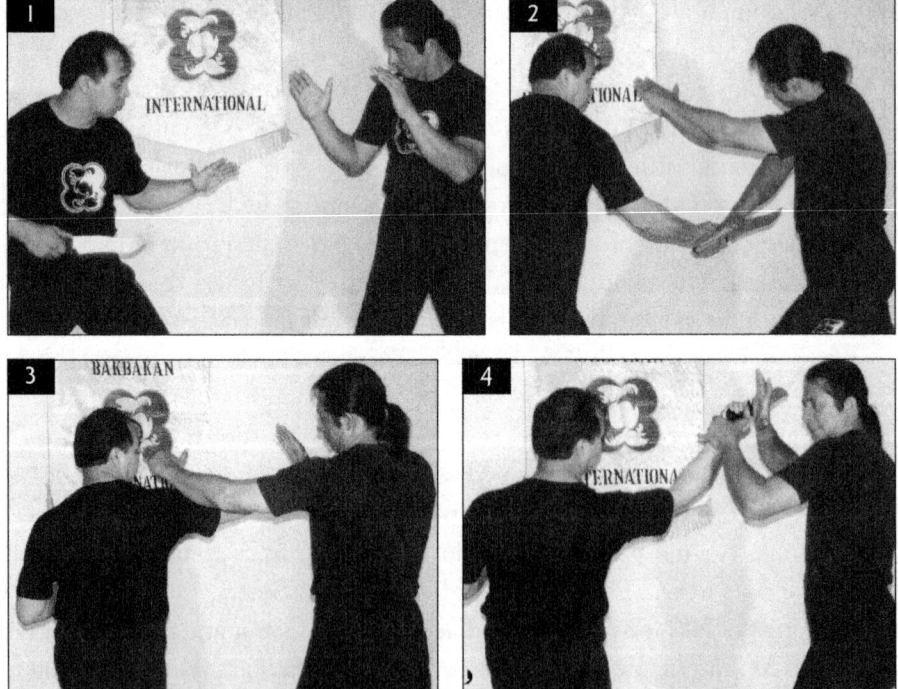

After a successful disarm, Diego maintains control of Rickett's arm while thrusting the knife into his throat (fig. 5). Diego completes the technique by applying an arm lock and head-control, repositioning the opponent and hindering his defensive capabilities, while finishing him off with another thrust to the throat (fig. 6).

*Tony Diego is the heir apparent to the kali system of Antonio Ilustrisimo.

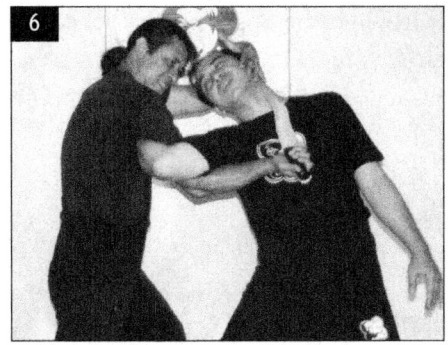

## Technique of the "Classical" Martial Art of the Lightning Scientific Arnis
Single Stick Vs. Stick and Dagger

Grandmaster Benjamin Luna Lema (right) prepares to defend against an attack (fig. 1). As the strike nears, Lema blocks it and checks the opponent's hand (fig. 2), en-route to tying up the opponent's attacking arm (fig. 3).

Although the opponent is locked, Lema is free to check and block the knife thrust (fig. 4). Lema finishes the technique by repositioning his body away from the knife and locking his opponent's limbs once again (fig. 5) and taking him down (fig. 6).

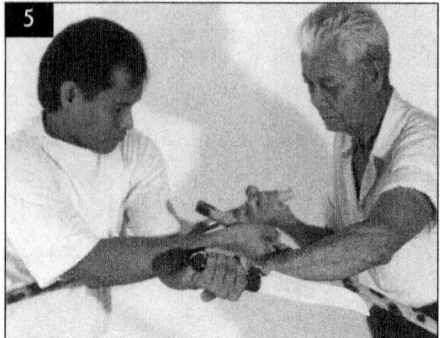
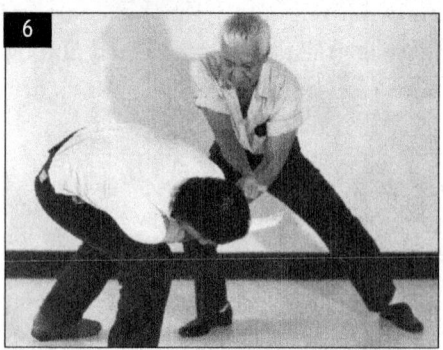

## Technique of the "Modern" Martial Art of Kuntao Lima-Lima
### Defense Against a Spinning Kick

As the opponent initiates a spinning kick, Grandmaster Carlito Lañada (left) prepares his defense by guarding his lower and upper body (fig. 1).

As the kick nears, Lañada pivots 90 degrees to the right and scoops the on-coming leg (fig. 2), then kicks out the opponent's supporting leg (fig. 3).

Lañada then sweeps the opponent while maintaining control of his right arm (fig. 4), and finishes with a reverse punch to his throat (fig. 5). *Photos courtesy of Carlos Aldrete.*

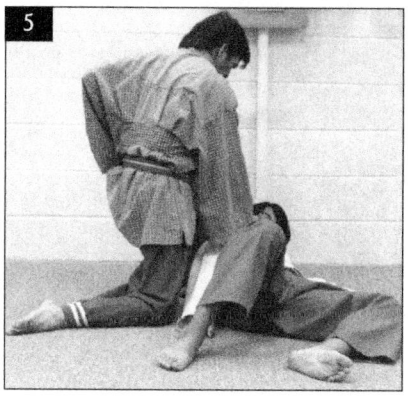

# Technique of the "Modern" Martial Art of Sikaran
## Defense Against a Crescent Kick

Master Jimmy Geronimo (left) squares off with his opponent (fig. 1). As the opponent executes an inward crescent kick, Geronimo parries it (fig. 2).

He then simultaneously grabs the opponent's extended leg to offset his balance, angles his body to the outside of the kick's direction of force, and counters with a roundhouse kick to the opponent's sternum (fig. 3).

As the opponent falls to the ground, Geronimo retracts his kicking leg in an effort to keep the distance between him and his opponent, to avoid being attacked by groundfighting techniques (fig. 4).

\* *Jimmy Geronimo is the brother of Grandmaster Meliton Geronimo, the developer of sikaran and current mayor of Baras, Philippines.*

**Ethos of Filipino Martial Culture**

The following discussion will highlight the core differences between the ethos of the contemporary Filipino warrior and the warrior ethic found in India, China, and Japan. The discussion attempts to show that as Asian martial arts in general have become more sophisticated, their techniques have become less effective in a strict martial sense, while becoming more "civilized" in the expressions of dance, drama, art, and sport competition. Moreover, it will be shown that, although the contemporary Filipino warrior (i.e., the masters) attempts to emulate this "higher form" of martial culture, he will be unable to fully assimilate it, relying more heavily upon the refinement of specific physical fighting techniques.

As the martial arts in the Philippines have moved from "ancient" to "classical" to "modern," its practitioners have attempted to emulate what they perceive as "higher" forms of martial culture (e.g., the adoption of training uniforms, colored-belt ranking, and structured group classes). This emulation began as a result of martial culture contact with Japan. However, while the martial cultures of these countries have become more passive through time, the Filipinos have apparently been unable to shed their warrior ethos. This is evident in the continuation of legal "death-matches" (*patayan*) until 1945, and their existence in private today—an event compounded by Filipino culture itself.

One does not find this kind of combative ethos present in India, China, or Japan. And while the Filipinos have attempted to emulate the evolution of martial arts as it is understood in these three countries, they have thus far been unsuccessful in doing so. However, unlike in India, China, or Japan, the Filipino has been able to maintain the martial rigor of true fighting disciplines.

Essentially, it may be postulated that the Filipinos have been unsuccessful in emulating "higher" martial arts forms as a result of the prevalent intensity of their warrior ethic. Whatever the impinging factor in Filipino culture—perhaps the self-concept of inferiority from being invaded and colonized by so many countries, or constant warring factions between islands—it is essentially a throwback to Japan's pre-Tokugawa period (1603-1868). During Japan's seventeenth century Tokugawa period, the military government (*bakufu*) organized the various warrior factions into a single unit (Donohue, 1991). This has not taken place in the Philippines. As a result, there is still no single martial arts organization, or political faction, or ethnic or social integration. In essence, it can be said that the Philippines is faced with having no essential original national character.

In contemporary Indian society, martial arts have become so diluted that they are virtually found only expressed in dance form. Even the classic work on the subject by Draeger and Smith (1980) merely focuses on its sport-oriented wrestling tradition. Zarrilli (1992) is the first American scholar to "rediscover" the existence of the ancient Indian martial art of kalarippayattu. But even his analysis of the combat form is in terms of physical fighting techniques as dance movements, and as an internal alchemy used to improve one's health—not to fight off warring factions or other martial practitioners. Therefore, not only has India's martial culture become diluted but it is virtually extinct.

On the contrary, the People's Republic of China has maintained its martial culture as a national treasure. This was done as a political vehicle to project the essence of its culture to the world. In the twenty to thirty years since the Cultural Revolution, members of China's politbureau have investigated their martial traditions. This was effected by insisting (against the will of the masters) that practitioners demonstrate in public and allow video taping of their skills. This permitted the Chinese Government to make a catalog of its broad martial culture (Maliszewski, 1992). As a result, the Chinese Government took archaic forms of combat and diluted them into a single, unified martial form known as *wushu* (Draeger and Smith, 1980; Maliszewski, 1992). Wushu combines elements of martial arts, dance, and opera with gymnastic overtones into the formation of a single expression of Chinese culture. Thus, as wushu, Chinese martial culture is at once more accessible and more easily comprehended by the outside world. One finds little effort made on behalf of the Philippine Government to preserve their martial culture.

Historically, the classical martial arts of Japan were relatively unknown even to Japanese citizens. To this day, the Japanese have been cited as having little knowledge of their true martial heritage (see Draeger and Smith, 1980; Maliszewski, 1992). In fact, the samurai tradition disappeared over 300 years ago. Draeger and Smith note that the martial arts (*bujutsu*) forms have been superseded by the martial way (*budo*) forms. Furthermore, even though specific fighting techniques of the bujutsu tradition were practiced in Japan, it was done so clandestinely (Donohue, 1991; Maliszewski, 1992). Moreover, while various martial arts are still practiced in Japan today, the actual intensity of feeling a need to kill somebody in a "death-match" as part of a routine test of skills is not found. While this warrior ethos was present in Japan during medieval times, it clearly does not exist in contemporary Japanese society.

Indian, Chinese, and Japanese cultures are able to maintain a consistency of information concerning their martial disciplines through the existence of "preserved" textual writings. The Filipinos have no such body of literature. What is found, rather, are a number of writings that have paraphrased common sources that are themselves largely inaccurate. Perhaps due to a heightened sense of cultural value placed on scholarship in other Asian countries, their martial arts are viewed in a more favorable light (see, for example, Alter, 1992; Sayama, 1986; Wile, in press). Conversely, as a result of invasion and constant repression of their indigenous beliefs, a general lack of literacy, and a general poor third-world image, Filipinos at large tend to look with disfavor upon their own cultural (and martial) heritage (see, for example, Maliszewski, 1992; Zaide, 1979).

It is a positive attitude toward martial culture that has led other Asian countries to further develop and refine their martial arts. This can be seen in the standardization of rank and its corresponding colored-belt designation, the opening of formal martial arts schools for public instruction, and recommended reading of indigenous philosophical works. These elements have further heightened the Indian, Chinese, and Japanese understanding of the warrior worldview that involves an intimate synthesis of Eastern philosophy and religion. In the Philippines, however, there is no unified or generally accepted martial arts ranking structure or formal schools of instruction. There is also no major indigenous religious tradition or philosophical ideology that embodies ancient and contemporary Filipino beliefs. What is found, rather, are various syncretic forms of endemic animistic beliefs, Islam, and Catholicism. Moreover, in the Philippines, the individual personal beliefs of an instructor may in fact have no direct relationship, correlation, or extension to a particular system or to the teacher his system is supposedly based upon.

Conversely, in countries like India, China, and Japan, one finds the imparting of knowledge of an art to generally embrace an entire system of physical skills, philosophy, and, in some cases, relevant supernatural practices and healing traditions. In these countries the whole of a system is transmitted from teacher to student—the student molding himself to the art through established ritualistic practices. This is not the case in the Philippines, where the individual is often looked upon as greater than the art, as evidenced by the vast number of systems named after contemporary grandmasters (see Table 1). Such belief patterns and practices are precisely why there is so much disunity among the various ethnic groups in the Philippines and why the central and northern regions were successfully colonized by the "divide-and-conquer" strategy employed by the Spanish conquistadores in the sixteenth century.

The Philippine Archipelago is a melting pot of peoples and cultures. While the evolution of Filipino martial arts may be interpreted by some in terms of ideas assimilated from its Asian neighbors, to do so solely in such terms is naive. As Harding (1960: 54) suggests: "When acted upon by external forces a culture will, if necessary, undergo specific changes only to the extent of and with the effect of preserving unchanged its fundamental structure and character." There is presently no single martial arts organization, or political faction, or ethnic or social integration in the Philippines. However, it is precisely the Filipinos' ability to absorb other cultural traditions without being absorbed that has crafted their martial arts into something essentially and uniquely Filipino.

It can therefore be concluded that while three classifications of Filipino martial arts exist today (i.e., "ancient," "classical," and "modern"), their contemporary practitioners appear to be moving toward completely embracing the "modern" form. The intent of these practitioners to follow the patterns that have unfolded in India, China, and Japan to promote commodified, government sanctioned martial "arts" and sports is apparent in the results of this study. While many of the contemporary grandmasters embody the ethos of the "ancient" Filipino warrior (e.g., the primary use of bladed weapons as opposed to sticks, the possession of amulets and prayers for divine protection in combat, and the belief that participation in a "death-match" is the only true indicator of one's skill), the practitioners of the modern systems do not. Therefore, it remains to be seen whether the social and political factors in the post-modern Philippines will continue to maintain a hold on any evolution of a cohesive unified martial arts ideology that complements its Asian neighbors.

## Acknowledgements

I would like to thank David M. Kutzik, Ph.D. for his help in determining the appropriate statistical procedure for this study and with its subsequent interpretation. I also wish to thank Michael Maliszewski, Ph.D. for his comments and suggestions with regard to my comparison of the ethos of Filipino martial culture with that of India, China, and Japan.

## APPENDIX
### Classification Methodology
by Mark V. Wiley and David M. Kutzik, Ph.D.

Unlike other Asian countries that have placed high standards on the documentation of their cultural heritage, the Philippines has not. As a result, reliance on written sources is an inadequate resource when attempting to classify the Filipino martial arts. This becomes evident when one considers that of the 35 books written on the subject, 30 draw their information from either one or both of two primary sources (i.e., Inosanto 1977; Yambao 1957). However, neither of these sources is truly accurate in their presentation or representation of the vast number of martial arts that are currently found in the Philippine Archipelago. (For a review of the literature on Filipino martial arts see Wiley, in press-b).

For the purpose of classifying the Filipino martial arts, it was necessary to conduct field research in the United States and the Philippines to meet, train with, photograph, videotape, and interview the leading practitioners of the arts. Twenty-one grandmasters participated in this study, among a host of masters and students. It should be noted that the interview respondents were not selected on the basis of popularity and purported skill level alone. Criteria for selection included the individual's age, experience, reputation, critical acceptance by peers, established lineage, verifiable history, demonstrable skill level, and general availability for a face-to-face interview and photograph and/or video recording session. The distinguishing factor that sets these grandmasters apart from the mainstream is that they are not mere grandmasters in a general martial art style, but grandmasters of a specific martial art system. A concerted effort was made to contact as many of these "headmasters" as possible. This allowed me to include 21 grandmasters representing an equal number of systems in this study (see Table 1).

Contact was made with the respondents included in this study in one or more of the following ways: 1) initial informal contact was made by way of verbal and/or written communication; 2) participation in private training sessions, group classes, and/or seminars was arranged; 3) travel to the masters' homes or schools to conduct interviews.

To facilitate the research process, an in-depth structured interview was constructed based on preliminary research findings in the written sources. Structured face-to-face interviews were then conducted that were tape recorded and the results transcribed by hand. The transcriptions were then transcribed to uniform data recording forms (see Table 2) and subjected to content analysis. Content coding was used to construct several variables to be used in a quantitative analysis: 1) time; 2) type; 3) region; 4) supernatural; and 5) foreignness. Each grandmaster's response was then recorded and coded on individual uniform data recording forms on which interview responses relative to each of the five variables were recorded by either circling a "0" (identifying no inclusion in their system) or a "1" (identifying inclusion in their system).

In addition, an inclusive library of the primary and secondary written sources on Filipino martial culture was collected. The written sources were then subjected to content analysis based on various scholarly, historical, and cultural references; subject interview responses; and participant observation. Rather than test hypotheses in the classical sense, correlation analysis was used to explore the patterns of clustering of indicators related to the three martial classifications: "ancient," "classical," and "modern." The reader should recall that, while others maintain that there is one unified art form, through analysis of physical martial maneuvers, types of weapons used, and region where the art was founded, it is evident that there are in fact 27 categorical systems that can be so classified into the three constructs of "ancient," "classical," and "modern."

The purpose of the correlations is to provide empirical verification of the meaningfulness of the three classifications of Filipino martial arts. It is expected that 1) the three types of classification would show weak or negative intercorrelations demonstrating their relative independence (non-overlap); and 2) that correlations with other items characteristic of the classifications but not included in the index would corroborate the relative mutually exclusive nature of the classifications. Thus, the correlations are not intended as measures of explained variance in the usual sense but rather as indicators of typological overlap or non-overlap.

The classification variables were constructed as three independent additive indexes: "ancient," "classical," and "modern." "Ancient" was operationally defined as the sum of four variables: 1) the primary use of Indonesian and/or Malaysian edged weapons; 2) the use of projectile weapons; 3) the use of flexible weapons; and 4) the use of elaborate geometric patterns around which footwork movements are structured. "Classical" was operationally defined as the sum of three variables: 1) the primary use of European-style edged weapons; 2) the inclusion of an elaborate hand-to-weapon defensive system but a marginal hand-to-hand defensive system; 3) the use of footwork patterns structured around a triangle set between parallel lines. "Modern" was operationally defined as the sum of three variables: 1) the inclusion of a hand-to-hand defensive system with techniques largely incorporated from Okinawan karate; Japanese karate, aikido, and/or judo; Korean taekwondo; and/or Chinese wushu; 2) the limiting of footwork to linear movements, if it is used at all; and 3) the training curriculum centered around modern sport competition. Thus, each respondent would have three scores, one for each of the classifications. In this way, respondents could have a mixed classification across categories.

Nonclassification variables used in the analysis included "region," "supernatural," and "foreignness." These variables were also constructed as three independent additive indexes. "Region" was operationally defined as the sum of three variables: 1) north (the island of Luzon); 2) central (the Visayan island cluster); and 3) south (Mindanao and the Sulu archipelago). "Supernatural" was operationally defined as the sum of four variables: 1) the possession of Christian amulets; 2) the possession of Islamic amulets; 3) the use of Christian prayers when fighting; and 4) the use of Islamic prayers when fighting. "Foreignness" was operationally defined as the sum of three variables: 1) the use of nonindigenous martial arts uniforms; 2) the teaching of classes in a rigidly structured, militaristic fashion; and 3) the integration of martial fighting techniques from any combination of Okinawan, Japanese, Korean, and/or Chinese martial arts. These were each coded as dichotomous categories with "1" indicating the presence of the trait or characteristic and "0" indicating the absence of the trait or characteristic.

Pearson correlations were produced using the SYSTAT statistical package. Several key points emerged that appear to support the conceptual classification of Filipino martial arts into "ancient," "classical," and "modern." As can be seen in Table 3, as one is more "ancient," for example, there is a slight negative correlation with being "modern" (-.245), a slight correlation with being "classical" (.204), and a perfect positive correlation to being from the south (.677). In addition, subjects found to possess either Christian or Islamic amulets and prayers (.320 and .519, respectively) were found to be from the south. Furthermore, the classification of "modern" is negatively correlated with emerging from the central Philippines (-.514) or southern Philippines (-.476), supporting the contention that those systems ascribed as modern originate on the northern island of Luzon. Other factors associated with the "modern" classification include a strong correlation with cross training (.719), the use of structured classes of instruction (.406), and the use of foreign martial arts uniforms (.374). The "classical" classification was found to be strongly correlated with central (.457), somewhat correlated with south (.356), but negatively correlated with north (-.204).

In addition to the correlations, a principle component analysis (Varimax model) with the number of factors set to three was produced. The results of the confirmatory factor analysis did in fact lend convincing evidence to corroborate the three conceptual classifications.

As can be seen in Table 4, the first set of results shows factor loadings where large positive coefficients demonstrate intercorrelation of the individual variables with the factor construct. By looking at the large coefficients (loadings) and working backwards to see which variables load strongly on each of the three factors, it is possible to identify Factor 1 as "classical," Factor 2 as "modern," and Factor 3 as "ancient." These charts give the name of the variable indicator plotted on a two-dimensional surface. Thus, the stronger the intercorrelation (factor loading) of the variable with others making up the factor, the closer together their names appear in the plot. There are three plots, each representing different views of the three dimensional cube plot representing the intercorrelation of all items with the three factors.

It is therefore evident that there exist three classifications and nine categories of Filipino martial arts—corresponding to specific time periods in Philippine history, regional island location, and technical fighting characteristics within which all of the contemporary grandmasters' systems may be categorized.

---

### TABLE 1
### Key Informants/Respondents

| Contemporary Grandmasters | Martial Arts Systems |
|---|---|
| 1. Herminio B. Biñas, Sr. | Biñas Dynamic Arnis |
| 2. Angel Cabales | Cabales Serrada Escrima |

| | |
|---|---|
| 3. Ciriaco Cañete | Escrido |
| 4. Onofre C. Escorpizo | Arnis Pangasinan |
| 5. Ramiro U. Estalilla, Sr. | Rigonan-Estalilla Kabaroan |
| 6. Nes Fernandez | Arnis Fernandez |
| 7. Reynaldo S. Galang | Hagibis |
| 8. Meliton C. Geronimo | Sikaran |
| 9. Leo M. Giron | De Fondo Escrima |
| 10. Antonio Ilustrisimo | Kali Ilustrisimo |
| 11. Porferio S. Lañada | Arnis Lañada |
| 12. Carlito A. Lañada | Kuntao Lima-lima |
| 13. Benjamin Luna Lema | Lightning Scientific Arnis |
| 14. Amante P. Mariñas, Sr. | Pananandata Mariñas |
| 15. Remy A. Presas | Modern Arnis |
| 16. Christopher Ricketts | Sagasa |
| 17. Edgar G. Sulite | Lameco Eskrima |
| 18. Bobby Taboada | Balintawak Cuentada |
| 19. Samson Tendencia | Arnis Tendencia |
| 20. Raymond Tobosa | Tobosa Kali/Escrima |
| 21. Florendo M. Visitacion | Vee Arnis-jitsu |

**Selected Characteristics of Sampled Respondents**
n = 21 grandmaster of Filipino martial arts
Average Age = 63.38 years; Still Actively Teaching = 17
Residence: Philippines = 8; United States = 13

---

## TABLE 2
### Code Book of the Uniform Data Recording Sheet Type

**TYPE**

**Ancient**

| | | | |
|---|---|---|---|
| • Asian Edged Weapons | Asianedg | 0 | 1 |
| • Flexible Weapons | Flexible | 0 | 1 |
| • Projectile Weapons | Project | 0 | 1 |
| • Elaborate Geometric Footwork | Geofoot | | |

**Classical**

| | | | |
|---|---|---|---|
| • European Edged Weapons | Euroedg | 0 | 1 |
| • Hand-to-Weapon | Handweap | 0 | 1 |
| • Triangular Footwork | Trifoot | 0 | 1 |

**Modern**
- Hand-to-Hand (Jap., Kor., Okin.)    Handhand    0    1
- Linear Footwork    Linfoot    0    1
- Competition    Compete    0    1

**REGION** (where art was developed)
- North (Luzon)    North    0    1
- Central (Visayas)    Central    0    1
- South (Mindanao, etc.)    South    0    1

**SUPERNATURAL**
- Amulet (Christian)    Chramult    0    1
- Amulet (Islamic)    Islamult    0    1
- Prayer (Christian)    Chrpray    0    1
- Prayer (Islamic)    Islpray    0    1

**FOREIGN**
- Uniform    Uniform    0    1
- Structured Classes    Class    0    1
- Cross Training    Cross    0    1

## TABLE 3
### Pearson Correlation Matrix

|  | Ancient | Classic | Modern | North | Central |
|---|---|---|---|---|---|
| Ancient | 1.000 | | | | |
| Classic | 0.204 | 1.000 | | | |
| Modern | -0.245 | -0.512 | 1.000 | | |
| North | -0.224 | -0.204 | 0.406 | 1.000 | |
| Central | 0.224 | 0.457 | -0.514 | -0.791 | 1.000 |
| South | 0.677 | 0.356 | -0.476 | -0.298 | 0.429 |
| Chramult | 0.320 | 0.057 | -0.353 | -0.583 | 0.429 |
| Islamult | 0.519 | 0.026 | -0.390 | -0.400 | 0.316 |
| Chrpray | 0.320 | 0.057 | -0.353 | -0.583 | 0.429 |
| Islpray | 0.519 | 0.026 | -0.390 | -0.400 | 0.316 |
| Uniform | -0.462 | -0.593 | 0.374 | 0.309 | -0.472 |
| Class | -0.306 | -0.341 | 0.406 | 0.213 | -0.316 |
| Cross | -0.075 | -0.581 | 0.719 | 0.316 | -0.357 |

chapter 3

# Showing the
# Forms of Filipino Kuntaw Lima-Lima

by Steven K. Dowd

*All photographs courtesy of Stephen K. Dowd.*

When peace had returned to the Philippines at the end of World War II, the Lañada family decided to bring kuntaw out to the public. In hopes of getting this art recognized around the world, Amang Iban Lañada arranged to send his son, Carlito, to Olongapo city where the Americans had one of the largest U.S. naval bases (Subic Bay Naval Station) in the South Pacific. Iban thought that, with the Americans' help, the art would eventually spread and flourish outside the Philippines.

Thus, in 1958, young Carlito Lañada left his province and went to Olongapo to establish a kuntaw school. At first, local martial artists would not take the art of kuntaw seriously. Laughed at and challenged by other martial arts organizations, Lañada found the way rough and not very prosperous. Here was a young man wearing a red, white, and blue colored belt that his father had given him to represent a sixth-degree rank in an art that previously had been secret. The belt represented the colors of the Filipino flag and the nation's determination, courage, and freedom.

Kuntaw is a style of fighting that uses the natural weapons of the body for blocking, striking, kicking, and throwing. It utilizes the hands for balance, parrying, grappling, and throwing. The legs are used simultaneously with the hands, or separately, for powerful leg techniques from various angles, including kicking, jumping, sweeping, and stomping techniques. With the knowledge of using these bodily weapons in various combinations to attack or counter-attack, kuntaw is unlimited in its martial applications.

Carlito Lañada often talks of unity in the fighting arts, a unity in which all martial artists should have and show respect for each other's art, as a separate art, and for all arts as a whole. He has lectured on this belief most strongly.

Opening his first school on Fendler Street, he called it "The Philippine Kung Fu Kuntaw Association." He chose the term *kung fu* (*gongfu*) because it was becoming familiar to those interested in martial arts. In 1964, he moved his growing school to the Linda Theater, which had gone out of business, and renamed the school "Maharlika Kuntaw" (*Royal Blood Kuntaw*), the original name handed down from his grandfather, Yoyong.

The teachings were strict and very aggressive. Rattan sticks were not only used to train in traditional kali and kuntaw arnis, the kuntaw lima-lima style of weapons training, instructors also used the sticks when correcting a student's empty-hand movements. Training in the Linda Theater brought many students to kuntaw. Night after night when entering the school for training, the senior instructors would line up in the front rows, followed by row upon row of students. Once all were ready, Lañada would walk out onto the theater's stage so all could see him for instruction and commence the night's training.

The training started with exercises to loosen the body, followed by exercises to strengthen and stretch it. After these exercises, Lañada put the students through basic striking, blocking, and kicking drills. Then the instructors separated groups of students according to their ranks. Lañada constantly made the rounds to see that instructors were teaching each group correctly to develop coordination, balance, and power for each technique. Beginners worked at perfecting their basics; others worked on the flowing forms; and still others studied lima-lima stick-fighting, sport combat, or more advanced sparring techniques.

Lañada takes pride in getting kuntaw recognized on Luzon Island. In 1966, with the art spreading throughout the Philippines, he incorporated the name *Kuntaw ng Pilipinas* (Kuntaw of the Philippines). In 1968, he was acclaimed the youngest martial arts art/style founder in the Philippines.

In 1970, the Philippine Karate Association (PKA) was formed. It was Lañada's ideas that put the association into motion and he was recognized as one of the founding members and is a lifetime counselor and administrator. A unity of the martial arts began to be seen in the Philippines.

In the following years, Lañada received more honors for his work. He was honored by Senator Ambrocia Padillo at the Parlarong Pilipinas (Philippine Games) with a Commemorative Award. In 1974, Ferdinand Marcos singled out Lañada for his work in promoting kuntaw. With the awards came a regeneration of the art that opened doors to military agencies in the Philippine armed services and throughout the American bases. Kuntaw now has schools throughout the world in such places as Bahrain, Guam, England, Germany, the Arab Emirates, Yemen, Canada, and the United States, with offers and interest in bringing kuntaw to Russia since the early 1990's.

Once kuntaw became internationally taught and recognized, Lañada decided to found the International Kuntaw Federation in 1977. Lañada's father, Amang Iban Lañada, passed away in 1984, but not before seeing his son make his dream of kuntaw's recognition throughout the world come true.

In 1990, Carlito Lañada moved to the United States and for a few years resided in Virginia. Kuntaw was soon recognized on the East Coast as a formidable fighting art. In 1994, with the urging of his West Coast students, he moved to California where the art flourishes under his guidance and inspiration.

## KUNTAW'S
## SEVEN UNDERLYING PRINCIPLES

There are seven principles underlying kuntaw training and philosophy that, when consolidated in practice, are believed to bring the student to the deepest understanding of the art. One aspect cannot work without another.

- <u>Balance</u> (*Panimbang*). Without balance, the attitude or stance can never be effective. Balance is achieved only through correct body alignment. Keeping the feet in proper relation to each other, as well as with the body, helps maintain correct body alignment. Proper balance permits relaxation, speed, and ease of movement, as well as providing a mechanical advantage making tremendous power and force possible.

- <u>Coordination</u> (*Koordinasyon*). Coordination enables the individual to integrate all the power and capacities of the organism into effective action. Before movement takes place, there must be a change in muscular tension on both sides of the joint to be moved. The effectiveness of this muscular teamwork is one of the factors that determines limits of speed, endurance, power, ability, and accuracy.

- Endurance (*Resistensiya/Tatag*). Development is brought about by hard and continuous practice that exceeds normal psychological and physical states, producing temporary near exhaustion.

- Posture (*Tindig/Tayo*). Good posture enables a person to move with grace and ease and helps develop a strong foundation.

- Power (*Lakas*). Power equals force times speed. Learning to move with accuracy and speed creates power.

- Timing (*Tiempo*). Timing becomes a technique that takes advantage of the slight interval before an opponent can readjust to block or counterattack.

- Speed (*Bilis*). Distance divided by time equals speed. Speed differs from velocity in that speed indicates only the magnitude of the change and not the direction.

  > **Types of Speed:** 1) *Mental:* quickness of mind in what to select; the right moves to frustrate and counter the opponent. 2) *Perceptual:* quickness of the eye to see an opening to discourage the opponent enough to confuse him and slow him down. 3) *Alteration:* quickness, alertness, and ability to change direction in midstream, which involves control of balance and inertia.

## Sayaw
A dance which is done for ceremony,
entertainment, and pleasure.

## Sayawan
The act or action of performing the sayaw.
The movements in a form of martial art
that show and express the art of that style.

**The Importance of Sayawan**

During the Spanish occupation of the Philippines, all native fighting arts were banned. Therefore, masters (*dalubhasa*) and students went underground to train in their arts. The forbidden arts flourished and were skillfully exhibited in the *sayaw* (dances) of the *moro-moro*, a social-religious play dramatizing the triumph of the Christian Spaniards over the African Moors in Granada, Spain. The sayaw movements were thought of as entertainment.

Not just ritual movements or drills of basic kuntaw techniques, the sayawan (forms) comprise a vast repertoire of stances, blocks, strikes, and kicks executed according to kuntaw's laws of balance, speed, and rhythm. In the passing of information from *guro* (instructor) to student and from generation to generation, sayawan provide a link with the past, comprising valuable tradition in kuntaw's development. Equally important, they serve as a training method for the day-to-day drilling of kuntaw techniques.

Sayawan offers an immense challenge, that of reaching the state of perfection, even for a brief moment, that feels in complete harmony with one's surroundings. The flow of sayawan is not a simple matter: whether in form or flow, it does not develop of its own accord. Its development requires practice, perseverance, and discipline. The true kuntaw practitioner spends a year mastering one sayawan.

Combining the sayawan and the seven principles of kuntaw makes possible the unity of mind, body, and heart.

## SAYAWAN APAT
## FORM FOUR

**1.** Stable stance. **2.** Turn half-left; move the right foot back, left foot in front to form a back stance, execute an offensive blocking hammer strike (*salag bayo*) (right [soft] upper block/left hammer fist strike). **2-B.** Opponent in left forward stance (*tayong pasulong*) executes an upper lunge punch. Defender executes an offensive blocking hammer strike.

**3.** Adjusting the left foot in front, form a forward stance; execute a pressing palm block (*salag papalad*) with the right-hand, then a left back fist strike (*hampas kamao*). **3-B.** Application of picture #3. Opponent in the same stance executes a middle reverse punch. Execute a right-hand pressing palm block, followed by a back fist strike to the opponent's face.

**4.** Turn right; adjust the left foot in back, right foot in front to form a back stance, execute an offensive blocking hammer strike (left, soft) upper block; right hammer fist strike. **5.** Adjusting the right foot in front, form a forward stance, execute a left pressing palm block, then a right back fist strike.

**6.** Turn left; left foot in front to form a forward stance; execute a low blocking punch (*salag suntok*) (left open hand is blocking next to right fist). **6-B.** Application of picture #6. Opponent executes a snap kick. Execute a low blocking punch.

**7.** Adjust the left foot in front to form a straddle stance, execute a left arm block (*salag bisig*). **7-B.** Application of picture #7. Opponent then follows with a roundhouse kick. Execute an arm block.

49

**8.** Adjust the left foot in front to form a forward stance, execute a right pressing palm block, then a left back fist strike (left fist comes from above the head and out to the front). **8-B.** Application of picture #8. Opponent then follows with a middle reverse punch. Execute a right pressing palm block, then a back fist strike.

**9)** Move the right foot to the front to form a back stance, execute a double-hand block. **10)** Move the right foot next to the left foot, turn half-left; right foot moves back, left foot in front to form a cat stance; execute a left (soft) outside block. **11)** Raise the left leg, execute a front snap kick.

**12)** Left foot stays in front, move the right foot behind the left to form a cross-leg stance, execute a right middle punch. **13)** Turn right, move the right foot in front to form a cat stance, perform a right (soft) outside block. **14)** Raise the right leg, execute a front snap kick.

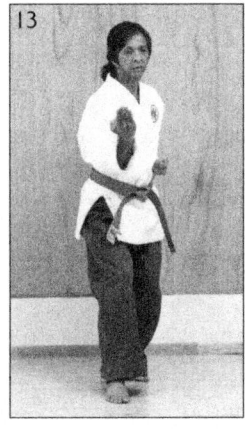

**15.** The right foot stays in front; move the left foot behind the right foot to form a cross-leg stance, execute a left middle punch. **16/16A.** Turn half-left; move the right foot back, left foot in front to form a snake stance (*tayong ahas*); execute a knife-hand block. **16-B.** Application of pictures #16/16A. Opponent executes a low snap kick. Move into a snake-stance, defensive position (knife-hand block), execute a pressing palm block.

**17)** Raise the body, left foot in front to form a forward stance, execute an offensive blocking chop (*salag pasibak*) (left [soft] upper block/right inside hand chop). **17-B)** Application of picture #17. Move into a forward stance, execute an offensive blocking chop.

**18)** Raise the right leg, execute a front thrust kick. **19)** Turn left (225° [45° left of centerline]); move the right foot back, left foot in front to form a forward stance; execute a (soft) wedge block. **20)** Raise the right leg, execute a front thrust kick.

**21)** Right foot moves in front to form a forward stance, execute a middle lunge punch. **22)** Execute a middle reverse punch. **23)** Execute an upper lunge punch.

**24)** Turn (45° right of the centerline), move right foot in front to form a forward stance, execute a (soft) wedge block. **25)** Raise the left leg, execute a front thrust kick. **26)** Move left foot in front to form a forward stance, execute a middle lunge punch.

**27-28)** Execute a middle reverse punch, followed by an upper lunge punch. **29)** Turn 45° left of centerline, move the left foot in front to form a back stance, execute a double-hand block.

**30)** Turn 45° right of centerline, move the right foot in front to form a back stance, execute a double-hand block. **31)** Turn 45° left of centerline, move the left foot in front to form a back stance, execute a double-hand block. **32)** Adjust the left foot in front to form a forward stance, execute a double inside hand chop.

**33)** In the same stance, make a grabbing motion with both hands (as if grabbing the opponent's head), execute an upward knee strike with the right knee (hands strike knee). **34)** Turn left 270°; move the right foot in back, left foot in front to form a back stance; execute a knife-hand block. **35)** Adjust the left foot, turn right, move right foot in front to form a back stance, execute a knife-hand block.

**36.** Move the right foot back next to the left foot to form a stable stance.

\* Editor's Note: Carlito A. Lañada is the founder of Kuntaw Lima-Lima, an art whose techniques are reminiscent of Okinawan Shorin-ryu and Shito-ryu karate styles, with underpinnings of Chinese gongfu. Grandmaster Lañada is adamant about not placing Filipino kuntaw in the same category as Chinese or Indonesian kuntao. In fact, as used here, the term "kuntaw" is an acronym comprised of the root words *kunsegrado* and *hataw*. *Kunsegrado* is derived from the Spanish words *con segrado* ("with sacredness") and the Tagalog word *hataw* (to strike). In Tagalog, *lima-lima* refers to the number five. Therefore, Kuntaw Lima-Lima is the art of "five sacred strikes," and has no connection to Chinese or Indonesian kuntao. Nor does it have any connection with the Muslims of Mindanao, who practice the Indonesian and Chinese kuntao systems.

**Special Thanks**
to sixth-degree
Lowell "Bud" Cothern
for his assistance in
the photo sequences.

chapter 4

# Philippine Arms & Armor in the University of Pennsylvania Museum of Archaeology and Anthropology

by Mark V. Wiley, B.S.

*University of Pennsylvania Museum (neg. #S4-141889)*

## Introduction

Exhibits of arms and armor in U.S. museums are few and far between. Most exhibits of the type focus on European medieval collections, and when one is presented on Asian weapons it usually focuses on those of Japan. Even rarer are exhibits of Southeast Asian weapons, and rarer still are those of the Philippines in particular.

However, some U.S. museums do have extensive collections of Southeast Asian weapons, including those from the Philippines. One such museum is the University of Pennsylvania Museum of Archaeology and Anthropology, located in Philadelphia. Although none of these materials are currently on display, the museum has in its storerooms nearly 1,000 martial artifacts from the Philippines, including swords, knives, spears, shields, helmets, and armor.

The museum building that houses these collections is an architectural masterpiece in its own right. The rotunda alone is a triumph of design: soaring twenty-seven meters over the grand paintings and sculptures of the Chinese gallery, it is one of the highest unsupported masonry domes in the United States. Noted architect Wilson Eyre, Jr. designed the museum in the 1890's in the North Italian Renaissance style, and the museums's eclectic decorative elements reflect the diverse cultures exhibited within. It is a lasting monument to the global vision that sent exhibitions to the far corners of the earth in the late nineteenth century.

Within the University Museum's walls, one will find an incomparable collection of archaeological and ethnographic artifacts, a record that covers thousands of years of human accomplishments across the whole of the inhabited world. A great number of these objects were acquired through the museum's own field research; more than three hundred expeditions have been sent out over the past one hundred years. However, the museum did not conduct its own fieldwork in the Philippines. The Philippine arms and armor in its collections were acquired as purchases or gifts from ethnographic collectors and from men who served in the Philippines during and after the Spanish-American War and in World War II.

**Philippine Slashing and Thrusting Weapons**

Historically, the ancient Islamic martial arts of the southern Philippines were taught and structured around the use of slashing and thrusting weapons. These weapons were often coated with various poisons prior to engaging in hand-to-hand combat. Moreover, Scott (1994: 148) notes that "the fiction that the metal itself had been rendered poisonous by some arcane alchemy no doubt enhanced its market value." Generally speaking, slashing and thrusting weapons were brought to the Philippines by way of Malaysia and Indonesia. In fact, the *kampilan*, a heavy dual-pointed sword, and the *barong*, a leaf-shaped sword, were originally weapons of the Sea Dayak people of north Borneo. Both of these swords have since been adopted as national weapons by the Philippine Moro of Sulu and Mindanao.

The Bornean Sea Dayaks believe that *Toh*, a powerful ghost-soul, resides in the heads of man. In times past, acquiring an enemy's head in combat through decapitation was a symbolic act of bravery, reconciliation, and revenge. However, once taken, Coe et al. (1993) note that the head "was treated with respect, cared for, and even fed." Because of its size and weight, the kampilan was the preferred weapon for head hunting. The kampilan has a carved hilt, a fork-shaped pommel, and a guard that stylizes the cavernous jaws of a crocodile. Kampilan are generally decorated with either red or black-dyed tufts of hair. The blade is long and straight with a single edge that widens to a dual-point.

Kampilan are sheathed in breakaway scabbards consisting of two pieces of wood shaped to fit the contour of the blade and fastened at two points with string or vine. This unique scabbard construction affords the warrior the ability to draw his sword and slash his opponent in one motion; at the initiation of a slashing motion, the string is severed and the scabbard falls apart, releasing the sword.

The University Museum's collection of kampilan is impressive. Shown in Figure 1 is a sample of six from Mindanao, southern Philippines (described here from left to right). The first kampilan shown with scabbard (#41-34-23 a/b) runs 99.8 cm from pommel to point, with a blade length of 74.2 cm and a scabbard length of 73.5 cm. The second kampilan shown with scabbard (#L-192-26 a/b) runs 106.3 cm from pommel to point, with a blade length of 79.6 cm and a scabbard length of 82.5 cm. The third kampilan with scabbard (#L-192-28 a/b) runs 98 cm from pommel to point, with a blade length of 71.5 cm and a scabbard length of 78.2 cm. It is interesting to note that the Philippine Constabulary confiscated both the second and third kampilan from the Moro of Lake Lanao, Mindanao. They were later collected by Lt. Col. Arthur Parker Hitchens and lent to the museum by Mrs. Hitchens. The fourth kampilan (#43-13-6) runs 96 cm from pommel to point, with a blade length of 71.5 cm. This particular sword was a gift to the museum from Mrs. Robert Ehrman in memory of her father, Major C. L. Beckhurts. The fifth kampilan (#16132) runs 86.5 cm from pommel to point, with a blade length of 62 cm. Interestingly, this kampilan was purchased in Spain by Stewart Culin in 1892 and deposited in the museum by C. Howard Colket in 1898. The sixth kampilan (#54-18-2) runs 83.5 cm from pommel to point, with a blade length of 67.5 cm. It was a gift to the museum from F. Lieber. Note that the pommel of this particular kampilan is different from the others. It is likely that the original handle had either broken, rotted, or was never made, and that the sword was fitted with a generic pommel by the collector or for a tourist.

The leaf-shaped barong is traditionally an indispensable part of Moro dress. Barong are carried in flat wooden scabbards decorated with elegant carvings, tucked in the front of the *sarong* (waist cloth). Barong were often an accompaniment of the Moro when engaging in the religious rite of *juramentado*[1] as enjoined in the Koran. Winderbaum (1977: 23) notes that barong were often etched with the following Arabic slogans: "There is no god but Allah" and "This barong has killed a score of enemies and must not be drawn from the scabbard except with intent to kill."

Barong often range from 40.5 to 45.5 cm in length and have simple pommels for fighting and elaborately stylized ones for ceremonial purposes. Whether simple or elaborate, the barong's handle is styled after the *kakatua* (cockatoo beak), which prevents it from accidentally slipping out of its wielder's bloody hand during combat. The slashing and chopping capabilities of the barong are difficult to match. Barong are the favored weapons for close quarter combat among Tausug, Samal, and Yakan warriors of the southern Philippines.

**Figure 1: Kampilan**
*University of Pennsylvania Museum (neg. #S4-141887)*

The University Museum's collection of barong is also quite impressive. Shown in Figure 2 is a sample of four barong from Mindanao (described here from top to bottom). The first barong shown with scabbard (#L-192-5 a/b) runs 48.5 cm from pommel to point, with a blade length of 34.5 cm and a scabbard length of 43.5 cm. This barong is from the Moro of Jolo Island, Sulu Archipelago. It was collected by Lt. Col. Arthur Parker Hitchens and lent to the museum by Mrs. Hitchens. Of special interest here is the German silver band found over the lower half of its wooden grip. The second barong with scabbard (#42-30-422 a/b) runs 57.4 cm from pommel to point, with a blade length of 37.3 cm and a scabbard length of 40.3 cm. This barong is from the Moro of Tawitawi, was collected by Casper W. Whitney and donated to the museum by Mrs. Morgan Wing. Of special interest here is the impression of a Chinese character just above the pommel on the facing side of the blade. The third barong shown with scabbard (#41-34-17 a /b) runs 63 cm from pommel to point, with a blade length of 40.3 cm and a scabbard length of 42.5 cm. The fourth barong (#54-18-21) runs 68 cm from pommel to point, with a blade length of 54 cm.

**Figure 2: Barong**
*University of Pennsylvania Museum (neg. #S4-141879*

Perhaps the most common sword found throughout Mindanao and Sulu is the *kris*. Traditionally, the kris is the great distinguishing ornament of all Malays. A symbol of royalty and power. Although kris are to be found in the Visayas, Scott (1994) notes that these are inferior to those from Mindanao and Sulu, which are less esteemed than imports from Makassar and Borneo. Like the barong, the kris is most extensively used by the Tausug, Samal, and Yakan tribes.

The origin of the kris is shrouded in mystery and has long been a matter of dispute among arms historians. One early theory posits that it derived from the *buntot pagi*, or stingray's tail. Some believe it was developed in the third century B.C.E. as a Hindu religious weapon with mystical powers. Others feel it has a Muslim background, as suggested by similar blades found in the Middle East, Indonesia, and Malaysia today. Still others assert that its design originates from the shape of the mythical *naga* (serpent or dragon).

Kris blades are forged from finely tempered steel of different grades, giving it the appearance of the revered Damascus blades. This forging method produces a blade with dark and light wavy lines called *pamor* (pattern). While ranging in length from 48 to 63.5 centimeters, kris are always double-edged. The blades are either completely straight (*sundang*), completely wavy (*kiwo-kiwo* or *seko*), or a combination of wavy at the bottom and straight at the top (*ranti*). A kris's shape and number of waves are significant, as they indicate its ethnic or regional origin. The pommels, made from such materials as hardwood, bone, antler, or shell, are stylized into a "horse-hoof" design known as *kalaw-kalaw*. Kris scabbards are called *taguban*.

The University Museum has an extensive collection of kris. Shown in Figure 3 is a sample of three kris (described here from top to bottom). The first kris shown with scabbard (#P1787 a/b) runs 58.5 cm from pommel to point, with a blade length of 48.3 cm and a scabbard length of 52 cm. It is from the Siassi Moro of Jolo Island, Sulu Archipelago, and was collected by Mrs. Helen Landell, who donated it to the museum in 1905. The second kris with scabbard (#L-192-13 a/b) runs 71 cm from pommel to point, with a blade length of 60 cm and a scabbard length of 64 cm. It is from the Moro of Cotabato, Mindanao; *Datu* (chief) Piang presented it to Col. Arthur Parker Hitchens on May 29, 1928, and Mrs. Hitchens donated it to the museum. The third kris with scabbard (#29-58-31 a/b) runs 78 cm from pommel to point, with a blade length of 66.5 cm and a scabbard length of 68 cm. While Mindanao Moro used this sword, it was apparently brought to the Philippines from the Malay Archipelago.

Perhaps the most basic and widely used sword in the Philippines is the long agricultural blade known as the *bolo*. Primarily a working tool, the bolo became famous during the Spanish-American War, when Filipino servicemen formed bolo battalions—troops armed with regulation firearms and bolo. The blades are generally rough or unfinished since they are made primarily for agricultural use.

### Figure 3: Kris
*University of Pennsylvania Museum (neg. #S4-141880)*

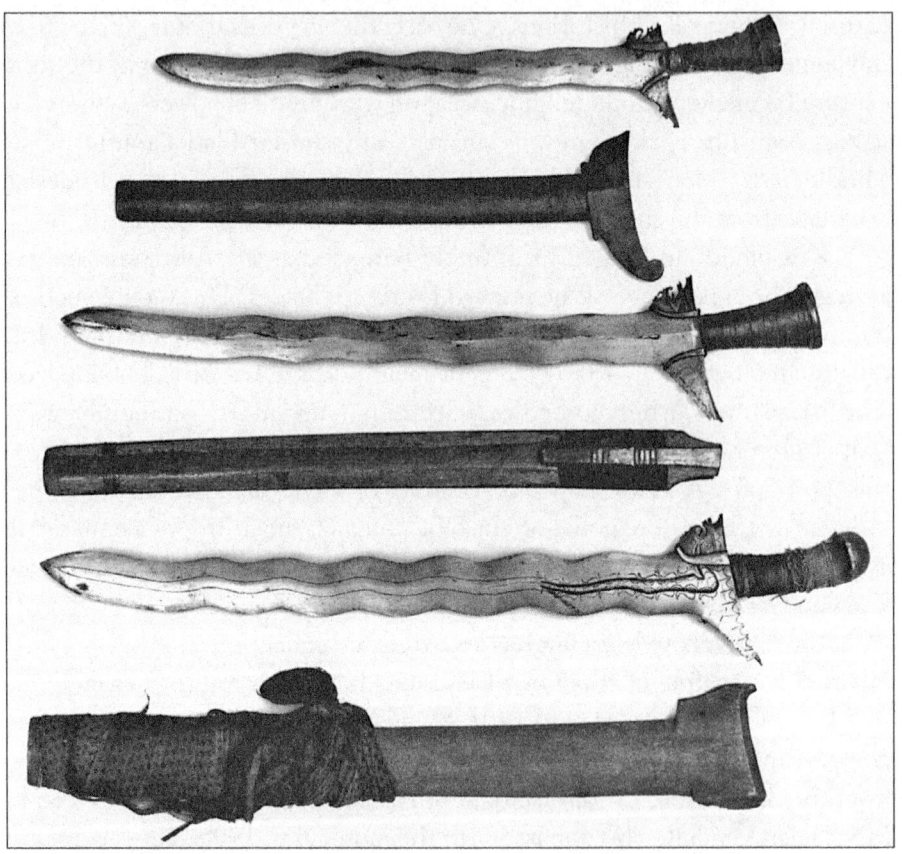

With the bolo's wide use, it is no wonder that the University Museum has a large number in its collection. Shown in Figure 4 is a sample of two bolo (described here from top to bottom). The first bolo shown with scabbard (#42-30-425 a/b) is from Iloilo, Luzon, and runs 45 cm from pommel to point, with a blade length of 33.2 cm and a scabbard length of 37.5 cm. The second bolo with scabbard (#42-30-392 a/b) runs 62.5 cm from pommel to point, with a blade length of 49.6 cm and a scabbard length of 52.4 cm. Both swords were collected by Casper W. Whitney and donated to the museum by Mrs. Morgan Wing.

### FIGURE 4: Bolo

*University of Pennsylvania Museum (neg. #S4-141886)*

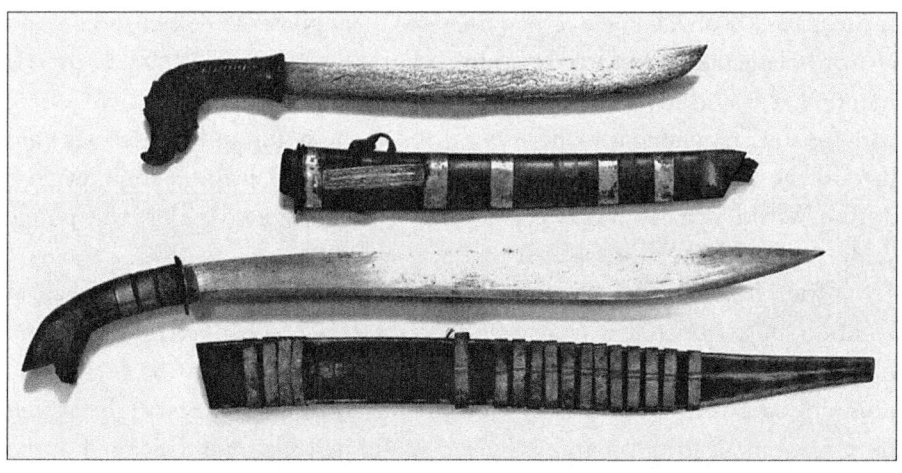

Another Malay slashing and thrusting weapon adopted by the Philippine Moro of Mindanao for combat is the *klewang*. This sword has a straight single-edged blade that generally widens toward its tip. The museum has only a few of these swords in its collection. Shown in Figure 5 are two klewang (described from top to bottom). The first klewang (#54-18-13) runs 64.5 cm from pommel to point, with a blade length of 49.5 cm, and was donated to the museum by F. Lieber. The second klewang (#29-9-21) runs 59 cm from pommel to point, with a blade length of 45.5 cm. This sword was collected by Col. Frank A. Edwards around 1900, and donated to the museum by Richard E. Norton in 1929.

### FIGURE 5: Klewang

*University of Pennsylvania Museum (neg. #S4-141881)*

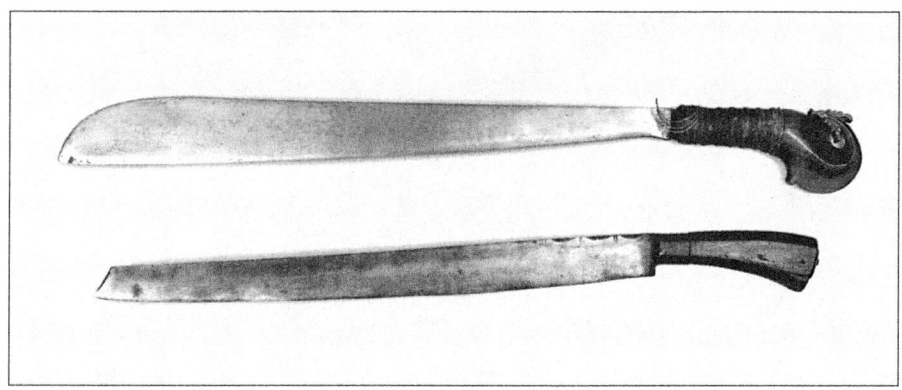

## A Chopping Blade

While the aforementioned weapons have both slashing and thrusting capabilities, there are also a few weapons used solely for chopping. For example, the *panabas* has a wide metal chopping head that appears to be a cross between a sword blade and an ax head. A jungle knife often used for executions, the panabas is popular in the Malabang, Cotabato, and Labuan districts of Mindanao. The panabas blade is widest near the point and bends backward toward the hilt. This chopper became a popular weapon for jungle warfare during World War II, and is perhaps a permutation of the Bornean jungle knife, *parang latok*.

The University Museum has a small collection of panabas. Shown in Figure 6 are two panabas from Mindanao, southern Philippines (described here from top to bottom). The first panabas (#16130) runs 85.5 cm from pommel to point, with a blade length of 53.5 cm. Interestingly, it was purchased in Madrid, Spain by Stewart Culin in 1892, and deposited in the museum by C. Howard Colket in 1893. The second panabas (#57-26-120) runs 73.5 cm from pommel to point, with a blade length of 41 cm. It belonged to Charles M. Small, a former military hospital steward who donated it to the museum on February 27, 1957.

**Figure 6: Panabas**
*University of Pennsylvania Museum (neg. #S4-141885)*

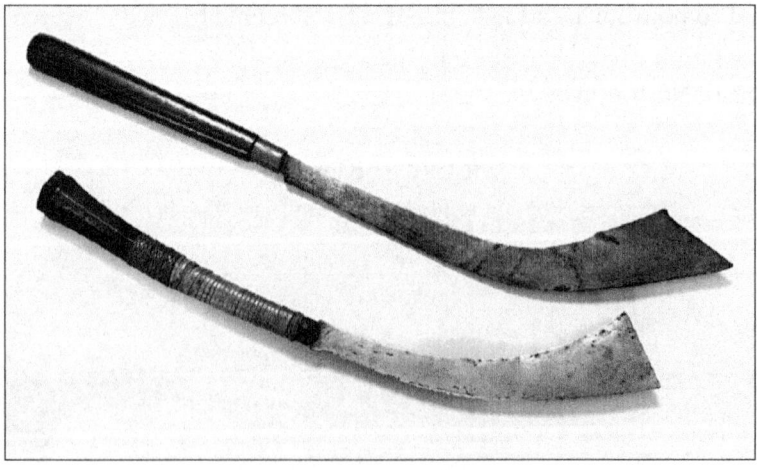

## Philippine Shields and Armor

For protection from an enemy's weapon, the Filipino warrior used various shields and, to a lesser extent, body armor. In general, the northern tribes' rectangular shields are characterized by five elongated points, two projecting down from the bottom and three up from the top. Northern shields are elaborate while southern ones are less so, with two or fewer projections, and they are often round or oval with no projections. With regard to the shields the Filipinos used during the Spanish occupation in the seventeenth century, Casiño (1982: 210) notes: "The fighting men carried shields called *taming*, which were large and circular; they were common in Sulu, Basilan, and among the coast dwellers in Western Mindanao. The highlanders used elongated ones called *kalasag*."

**Figure 7: Taming**
University of Pennsylvania Museum (neg. #S4-141889)

The taming is generally round and made of either woven rattan (*sawali*) or wood. The taming's origin is uncertain. Goquingco (1980) postulates that it may have come from the *tagbanwa* shield of the Muslim Maranao, and might be of Chinese origin; whereas Scott (1994) suggests that it may have been copied from those of the Moluccans or Spaniards.

The University Museum has only a few taming shields in its collection. Shown in Figure 7 is a wooden taming (#P 2976 B) with a thin piece of metal wrapped around its edge and a diameter of 86 cm. It is from the Bagobo tribe of Davao, Mindanao. The museum purchased it from the collectors, Misses Elizabeth H. and Sarah S. Metcalf, in 1914.

A *kalasag* is made of fibrous wood reinforced with woven rattan and is able to fend off most swords. However, its primary function was to protect its bearer from spears and arrows. Since the shield's material was fibrous, it was able to enmesh the enemies spear, thus preventing him from retrieving it. Kalasag can be found in any number of different sizes, although they are always nearly rectangular.

The University Museum has a nice variety of kalasag from both the northern and southern Philippines. Shown here are three kalasag, two from Luzon and one from Mindanao. Figure 8 is a kalasag (#50-49-64) of the Kalinga tribe of northern Luzon. It has a length of 129 cm and a width of 29 cm. The shield's two prongs at the bottom allowed its bearer to stand placing his lead leg between the prongs, and be guarded from mid-thigh to head. The prongs at the top allowed him to view the enemy, and the tapered shape allowed him to throw his spear without having to move his shield from its protective position. Figure 9 shows a child's kalasag (#5049-78) of the Tuit (Apayao) tribe of northern Luzon. It has a length of 90 cm and a width of 39 cm. Shown in Figure 10 is a kalasag (#P2977 a) of the Bagobo tribe of Davao, Mindanao. It has a length of 102 cm and a width of 54.5 cm. The museum purchased these shields from the collectors, Elizabeth H. and Sarah S. Metcalf, in 1914.

## Kalasag

**Figure 8** (left) *University of Pennsylvania Museum (neg. #S4-141884)*
**Figure 9** (right) *University of Pennsylvania Museum (neg. #S4-141888)*

**Figure 10 : Kalasag**
*University of Pennsylvania Museum (neg. #S4-141696)*

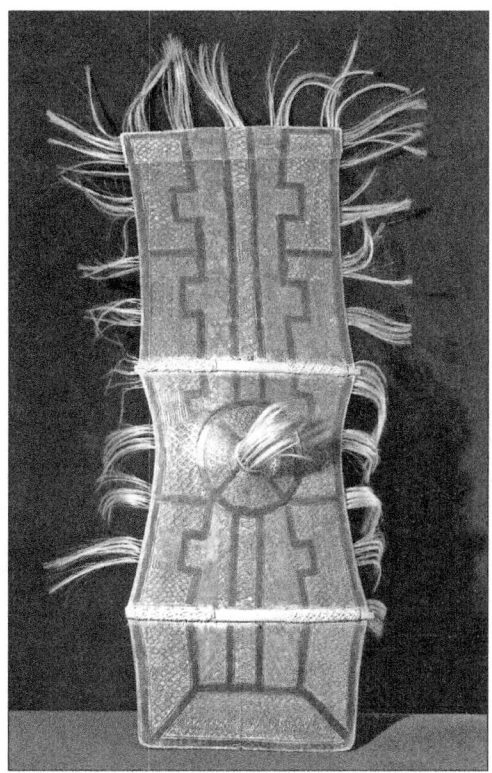

Although the native Filipino warriors (*mandirigma*) did not have European chain-mail armor, they did have a quilted equivalent called *barote*. Made of abaca cord woven tightly into braids, barote body armor is similar to modern-day ripstop nylon in that, when punctured, it will not tear due to its intricately woven pattern. The more solid body armor, possibly fashioned after the Spanish design, is *pakil*. Scott notes that in the Visayas, pakil was made of bark, bamboo, or *kamagong* (a hard wood), while in Mindanao it was made of carabao horn or elephant hide, and known as *baluti*.

Considering the scarcity of body armor that was actually used by Filipinos in battle, it is fortunate that the University Museum has one example in their collection. Shown in Figure 11 is pakil armor (#81-4-1) with a length of 67 cm and a width of 48 cm. It is believed to have been made by Moro in the late nineteenth to early twentieth century. The chain mail, silver locks, and ornamentation are believed to have been taken from Spanish armor and reworked into the piece. Mrs. F. Gardner Cox donated this pakil to the museum on April 10, 1981.

**Figure 11: Pakil**
University of Pennsylvania Museum (neg. #S4-141882)

In addition to shields and breastplates, Filipino warriors of Luzon also wore wooden helmets known as *kupya*, although they do not appear to have been widely used. Shown in Figure 12 are two kupya displayed to show their inside and outside construction. The helmet on the left (#50-49-262) is 18 cm wide with a depth or height of 12 cm. The helmet on the right (#50-49-263) is 19.7 cm wide with a depth or height of 11 cm. These kupya are from the Bontoc of Luzon.

**Figure 12: Kupya**
University of Pennsylvania Museum (neg. #S4-141883)

**Afterword**

I feel fortunate to have been granted permission to study the Philippine arms and armor collection in the University of Pennsylvania Museum of Archaeology and Anthropology. It is hoped that this preliminary review of their collections will foster an interest in this relatively unexplored field. Scholars pursuing research in the area of Philippine arms and armor may contact the museum for further information.

[1] During the religious rite of *juramentado*, a Moro would pray and then run through the streets swinging his sword and killing all the non-Muslims in his path. It was believed that the more he killed, the higher his seat in heaven, and his own death during the juramentado actually ensured his place in heaven.

## References

Casiño, E. (1982). *The Philippines: Lands and people, a cultural geography.* Philippines: Grolier International, Inc.

Coe, M., et al. (1993). *Swords and hilt weapons.* New York: Barnes and Noble, Inc.

Goquingco, L. (1980). *The dances of the emerald isles.* Quezon City, Philippines: Ben-Lor Publishers.

Horne, L. (Ed.). (1985). *Introduction to the University Museum.* Philadelphia, PA: University of Pennsylvania Press.

Scott, W. (1994). *Barangay: Sixteenth-century Philippine culture and society.* Quezon City, Philippines: Ateneo de Manila University Press.

Szanton, D. (1973). Art in Sulu, a survey. *Sulu Studies*, 2, pp. 2-69.

Wiley, M. (1997). *Filipino martial culture.* Tokyo: Charles E. Tuttle Co.

Winderbaum, L. (1977). *The martial arts encyclopedia.* Washington, D.C.: Inscape.

chapter 5

# The Art of Conversation:
# Random Flow Training in Visayan Corto Kadena Eskrima

by Maija Soderholm, B.Sc.

*Visayan Corto Kadena Eskrima is the name Sonny Umpad has given to his martial art system. Visayan refers to the Visayan Islands of the central Philippines where Umpad grew up. Corto Kadena means "short chain," and has many levels of meaning from the physical to the philosophical. Eskrima has the same root as the word "skirmish," therefore it can be loosely translated as "fighting art."*

## Introduction

This chapter is about the art of Visayan Corto Kadena Eskrima and some of its concepts and training methods with regard to free-sparring with swords. It is a Filipino martial system encompassing empty-hand and non-bladed and bladed weapons. Its principles, however, are based on the sword. It is essentially a dueling art that, in times past, would leave only one participant standing.

Unlike empty-hand or even stick fighting, dueling with swords offers no forgiveness. A mistake in timing or reaction does not lead to a bruise or a broken arm, but to severed tendons, deep trauma, and potentially death. A much greater emphasis is therefore placed on strategy than perhaps would be with less lethal weapons.

As those who spar with weapons know, to hit a target is not too difficult, but to hit a target and "get out clean," without taking a hit, is much harder. However, this must be the goal. Thankfully, today we do not have to prove our skill in challenge matches with live blades, but dueling in the traditional manner with non-lethal blades is still a valuable and fascinating lesson in human interaction, the training for which not only works the physical body but the mental/emotional and perhaps the spiritual as well.

The techniques, entries, strikes, and counters needed to prevail in a duel are as numerous as the variety of opponents one can meet. Rather than go into detail about all of these aspects, this chapter will focus on three fundamental skills, universal in nature and particularly pertinent to sword fighting, that underlie the Corto Kadena system. These are:

- The ability to understand relative motion and extrapolate from it.
- The ability to be accurate.
- The ability to differentiate a real threat from a feint.

- **Relative motion:** the way that two people interact in an attempt to gain an advantageous position from which to strike, while maintaining a defensive wall.
- **Striking:** involves choosing the position, angle, and timing from which a strike must be done in relation to the opponent's motion and position.
- **Ability to extrapolate:** understanding how the human body moves over time and understanding at each moment, the available options for stepping, weight shifting, and striking.
- **Accuracy:** refers not only to the ability to strike a chosen target, but to accuracy in judging range, differentiating angles of attack, and the ability to "catch" an opponent's rhythm.

Internalizing these concepts comes from partner practice, by watching others move in relation to oneself, and experiencing the potential actions and reactions as the motion unfolds. Understanding gained through a dynamic, free-form interaction with a partner will train the body to respond appropriately in real time by learning to recognize patterns and rhythms in movement. The Corto Kadena system trains these skills using the concepts of "pendulum motion" and "random flow." A pendulum has the quality of continuous motion. The two still points at either end of the swing come at the cusp of a deceleration and an acceleration and are only momentary. Pendulum motion ebbs and flows, gives and takes, but always re-cycles its energy.

There are three main pendulums: 1) the stepping pendulum, 2) the body pendulum, and 3) the weapon pendulum. In the beginning, the pendulums are practiced in a straight line, either with a swinging target or with a partner. The idea of moving in relation to something else is key. Accuracy in judging range, angle, and timing are trained and the changing position of the defense line in motion is explored.

**1-a-b Weapon Pendulum:** The weapon extends away from and back to the body. Also practiced side-to-side. *All photos courtesy of Maija Soderholm.*

Through practice, the motion becomes more natural and the pendulum becomes more free-form, circling around, changing lead, and moving side-to-side in no pre-determined pattern. The rhythm can change from slow to fast to slow again, but does not stop. This is Random Flow Training.

At this point, more subtle skills are introduced, including mirroring an opponent's movement (*salamin*), shadowing behind a strike (*anino*), and the use of body language to open the defensive line (*hata*).

Random Flow training is done at varying speeds, increasing with skill level. However, even highly skilled players practice at slow speeds to explore new angles, entries, and counters. The ability to keep continuous motion and accuracy of strike angle at low speed without stops, hesitations, or tracking will increase understanding of motion in real time.

Ideally, a videotape of a slow speed flow put on fast forward will look natural and real. Practicing at slow speed will also help with blade and body expression—a key element of successful feinting—and also with balance; hence the ability to issue power at any moment by exploring ways to coil and uncoil the body using high/low, left/right, and turning motions.

Like good conversation, Random Flow training is an interaction between two people where one speaks and the other listens and reacts dependent on what the first has said. This give and take will open up new angles of inquiry and new ideas to explore. The more open one is to another's questions, the more one is likely to learn.

Of course, dueling is different. It is competitive and non-cooperative. Flow, if any, happens before contact, after which the end game follows soon after. However, if our goal is to prevail in such an interaction, it is well worth our while to "converse" as widely as possible in our training, for the only true knowledge is experience. Training the eyes to see things for what they truly are, to evaluate the novel and unexpected, and respond appropriately is the best way to stay alive.

Fighting techniques using bolo knives— a standard issue knife for Philippine marines.
*Photographs by Defense Video and Imagery Distribution System. www.dvidshub.net*

# TECHNICAL SECTION

**2-a-c Body Pendulum:** The weight shifts from one leg to the other, forward and backward as shown. Shifting can also be side-to-side.

**3-a-c Stepping Pendulum:** Stepping pivots the body 180 degrees. For a Right Side Pendulum, the left foot stays as a fixed point and the right foot moves (opposite for Left Side Pendulum). The weight stays on the balls of the feet to facilitate pivoting. A change in direction can be executed from the central or neutral position (3-b), to encompass all 360 degrees of movement. Note how the opponents mirror each other's movement. The ability to syncopate these three pendulums is a key skill in flow training.

**4-a-d The Defense Line in Motion:** An understanding of how to maintain a defensive "wall" relative to a moving opponent means one can stay in range longer instead of backing away out of range and having to re-enter.

**5-a-c "Mirroring" (salamin):** By mirroring an opponent's blade and body angle, one protects the targets closest to their blade position, thus closing the most accessible targets they are in a position to strike.

**6-a-e "Shadowing" (anino):** By adding the subtlety of timing to mirroring, one can "slip" an opponent's strike and enter behind their defensive line.

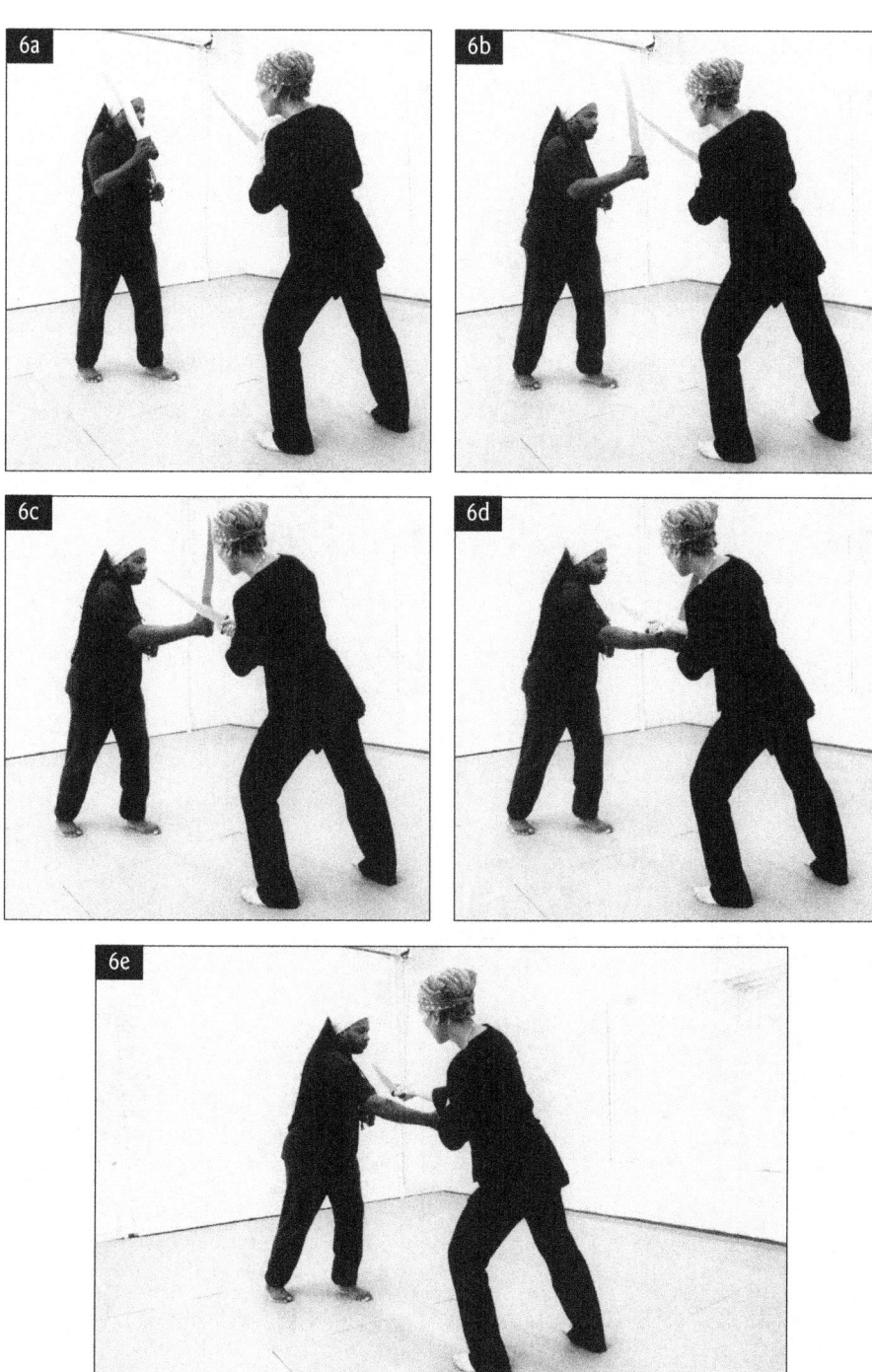

**7-a-d "Feinting" (hata):** Feinting requires a "feed" to cause the opponent to respond. If the response creates our opening, one can recreate the same feed later with the body, however, this time using a strike angle aimed at the opening. In the sequence below, a threat to the opponent's sword arm causes an overextended block to the right. Later, the same body angle is fed, however the blade is now directed at the opening on the left side.

**8-a-d Feinting Variation:** Feinting can also draw the opponent into making an attack, thus making an opening. An overly long cut invites a strike to the right ribs. Once the opponent has committed, a pivot out of range creates an opening for a cut to the underside of their weapon arm.

**9-a-e Coiling To Issue Power:** In the previous sequence (8-a-d), a pivot combined with a weight shift to the back creates a powerful pulling or whipping motion. The power is created by stepping behind and pivoting on both feet, creating an unwinding motion through the body and accelerating the blade.

## 10-a-l: Random Flow "Conversation"

**Acknowledgment**
A special thanks to Kenneth Ingram for
appearing in the technical section with the author.

chapter 6

# Remy Presas Remembered:
# A Perspective on Life in the Martial Arts

by Peter Hobart, J.D.

Professor Remy Amador Presas (Dec. 19, 1936-Aug. 28, 2001).
*All photographs courtesy of Peter Hobart.*

## Introduction

During the 1980's, a decade that epitomized selfishness in many ways, something truly remarkable happened in the North American martial arts community. In the midst of fierce competition among the various martial styles, schools and organizations, a group of grandmasters—all recognized experts and innovators in their particular disciplines—banded together to share ideas, techniques and seminars with each other. The result was that their students the world over enjoyed a breadth and depth of instruction unparalleled in common experience. The ancient fighting arts of Japan, China, Okinawa and the Philippines blended together in a chorus that preserved the distinctiveness of each voice but combined to produce a four-part harmony the strength of which truly exceeded the sum of its parts.

As one of those fortunate enough to witness this phenomenon, I resolved long ago to interview each of the remarkable members of this extraordinary union, to compare their thoughts and experiences on a variety of subjects. To my great shame, I failed to act on this good intention before the unthinkable happened—one of the founding members, Professor Remy Amador Presas, died somewhat unexpectedly, and the circle was forever broken.

Many years ago, there was a weekend seminar in Philadelphia for which Professor Presas arrived a few days early. I was honored with the job of escorting him around the area in the interim, and had the opportunity to talk, train, and take meals with him one-on-one. I still recall many of the things we discussed and practiced vividly, but others are beginning to fade with time. Having only recently completed the other interviews I had committed to undertake so long ago, it seemed like the right time to commit to paper the words of Professor Presas that still remain available to me through fragments of old videotape, handwritten notes, fading memories and the kind assistance of those who contributed their own stories to this project.

### TOPICS

- **On being a teacher:**

The issue with which the Professor seemed most preoccupied in the days leading up to the seminar referenced above was what he called "presentation" or "profile." Some people consider the ability to inspire and engage others to be a useful tool in the event that they choose to be teachers. To hear the Professor tell it, these people had it backwards. The very having of such natural gifts, it seemed to him, required their possessors to teach others—presumably any subject matter, but preferably arnis.

"Some people", he explained, "have natural presentation, natural profile… they must teach it, you know."

Professor Presas taught people of all ages and backgrounds. Here a young practitioner utilizes his cane to elbow-lock Professor Presas.

- **Regarding the flow:**

The other thing that seemed to be uppermost in the Professor's mind on the occasion described above was the exercise known as "*tapi-tapi*." I picked him up at his hotel, and no sooner had I walked in to his room than he handed me an arnis stick and said, "strike it at me here, pamalo—with the cane." Unsuspectingly, I complied. The next thing I knew, there was a whirlwind of activity from the Professor, and I found myself disarmed, my forearms entangled with one another, and him laughing heartily. "What was that," I ventured? "We call it the *tapi-tapi*," he replied. "I will explain it to you more, but first, we eat!"

On the way to the dojo, the Professor rejected several fast food options, deciding instead on a trip to the produce aisle of the local grocery store. Half an hour later, armed with a variety of fresh fruit, and a martial arts dagger, he made for us one of the best fruit salads I have ever tasted, which we consumed together, sitting cross-legged on the dojo floor.

Afterward, the lesson continued. Like a tidal wave, the Professor's technique surged against my ineffective defenses, forcing me up and back along the length of the dojo. Blending seamlessly with some of the older and more familiar exercises was this "innovation of the *tapi-tapi*." He flowed from attack to counter to disarm so rapidly and flowingly that it was clear that this was an instinctive rather than a conscious application of technique. When the lesson had ended, the Professor smiled broadly and said, "this is the flow." At the time, I thought he meant the moves themselves. Many years later, I think I'm beginning to understand his meaning.

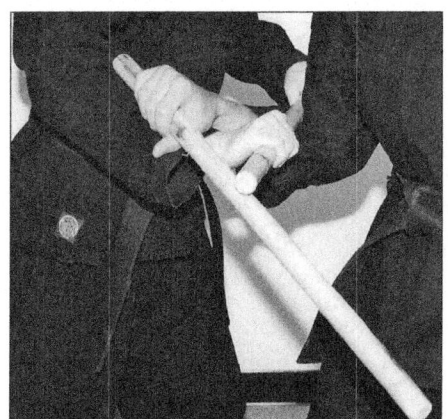 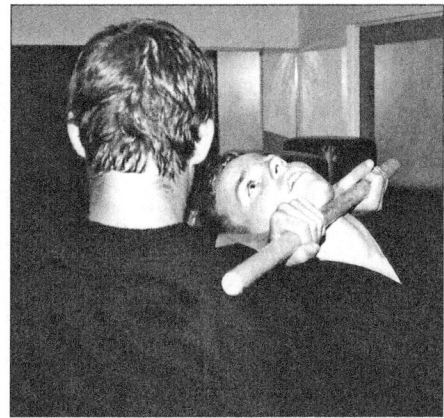

Wrist-lock and choke: two finishing techniques employed after exchanging multiple strikes and parries in the two-person "tapi-tapi" drill.

Left to right:
Dr. Charles Terry, Leo Fong, George Dillman, and Wally Jay, circa 1997.

- **In the words of his colleagues:**

**WALLY JAY:** "When Remy was teaching sometimes I might jump in, but I don't know his art. When I would show a guy, Remy would say, "you know it, you know the arts. It's the principle that's important."

**GEORGE DILLMAN:** "Remy—I miss him badly. I always tell people that he was my booking agent. Remy would call me: "you and I will teach a seminar. We will do this in Atlanta, Georgia." I'd go, "we will?" He'd say, "yes, yes, you must be there", and then he'd hang up! And he did the same thing with Wally and we put the three of us together, and that became awesome for almost fifteen years."

**LEO FONG:** "I trained with Remy for a year in 1974 when I was in the Philippines to do two movies. I lived there for an entire year. Remy would show up at my apartment every morning at 7:00 am. Sometimes I am still in bed when he knocked on the door. We would train for an hour, sometimes we would spend the day together riding in taxis and jeeps to go to different places such as cafés and movie studios. As far as martial arts is concerned I learned about flow and taking the total approach. Remy was not just about sticks, but the entire spectrum of martial arts. Although my personal preference is to develop and design my own approach; watching Remy did inspire me to go "outside the box". This is why I do not teach specific techniques from all the teachers I trained with such as Remy, Angel Cabales, Bruce Lee, Jimmy Lee, etc... A great teacher is one who points the finger to the door; but does not enter with the student. I have been fortunate to meet Remy and others who were great teachers because of that. They taught me to fish rather than just giving me a fish. In the process I also discover the "how" on my own. I remember Remy as a very giving person who was so anxious to share his art. Day one when I met him he was bubbling with enthusiasm. The first thing he asked after a short introduction was: 'When can we start training?'"

**DR. CHARLES TERRY:** "I was very fortunate to spend years attending seminars and camps of Professor Presas. I especially treasure the several months we spent traveling to seminars together after I finished Medical School. One aspect of his character will always stay with me: Professor Presas loved sharing. He shared techniques and concepts with martial artists of every background and level. Part of what made Modern Arnis spread so far was the Professor's openness to all students. He treated beginners and advanced students with equal respect and attention. The Professor took a personal interest in everyone he met. He made it a point to the remember people's names and faces. He met my family and always inquired about their health and happiness. He was one of the first people to send me a wedding present when I told him I was engaged. Once while we were on the road, I asked him where I could get one of the special Modern Arnis uniforms. He promptly removed his uniform top and said, "Doctor Terry, I want you to have this." He quite literally gave me the shirt off his back!"

Professor Presas and George Dillman
practicing techniques of Modern Arnis.

**CHARLES TULANE:** "What I think many observers missed was that Remy could set you up so thoroughly that he knew, with certainty, what you were going to do before you did it. And when he wanted you to do something, he knew not just how to make you do it, but often how to make you want to do it, commit to it, and think that you were doing a good thing. This is the set up that many players are lacking today. Too often you hear, "you can't do that; it isn't in the drill." This is wrong in my view. Remy never said, "you can't do that." He always had an answer to the unpredicted move, but, much more important, he rarely got unpredicted moves; he got the responses he did by very carefully calculating and setting them up.

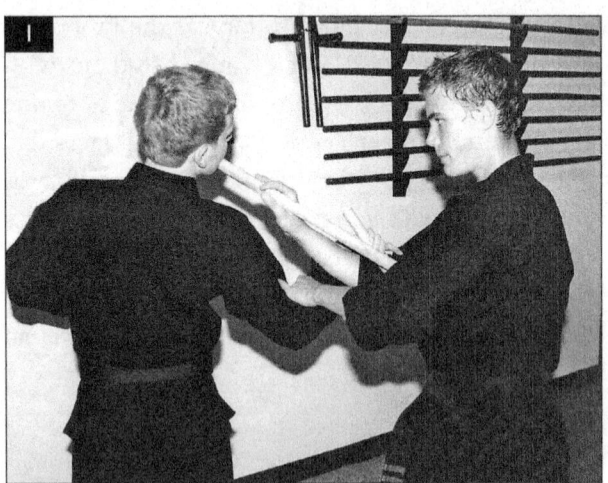

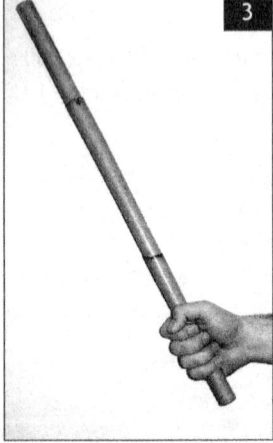

1) Jake Eckhardt and David Kerkeslager practice striking with the punyo. 2) Executing basic strike to the forehead or eye. 3) The proper way to hold the arnis cane, with sufficient *punyo* extending below the grip for striking or hooking.

Remy had some truly phenomenal attributes: amazing grip, super body mechanics, timing the ability to read and set up an opponent. In many ways he would slow moves down, but also change the structure of them to make them easier to follow and learn. For example, he would show things much larger than they needed to be so people could see, but he would also isolate out things like footwork. Some observers have commented that Modern Arnis seems to lack the characteristic triangle footwork of the Filipino martial arts. This clearly isn't the case; it is just that Remy would rarely move more than he needed to, and he could, and did, run bigger, stronger partners all over the room using these almost baby steps.

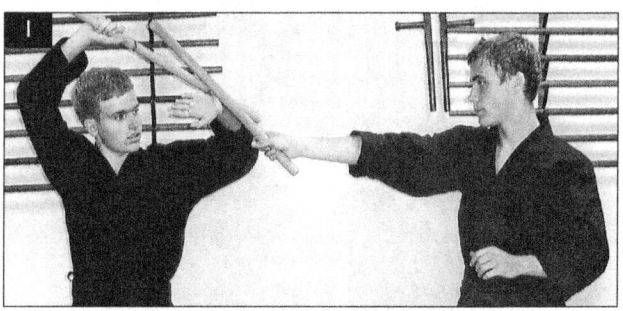

1) "Umbrella block": a warding-off defense from an overhead strike. 2) Reverse *sinawali* (weaving): a two-person drill in which each of several strikes is met with a mirror-image counter-strike by one's partner. 3) *Redonda* (whirlwind): a drill to practice a continuous flow of strikes.

But Remy's success really, I think, hinged on a single attribute; he could make every last person at a seminar feel like they were the focus of everything. He made sure that no one was left behind, and he made sure everyone caught some of the joy he exuded when he taught. Everyone left with something they didn't have when they came, whether they were brand new or had twenty years in."

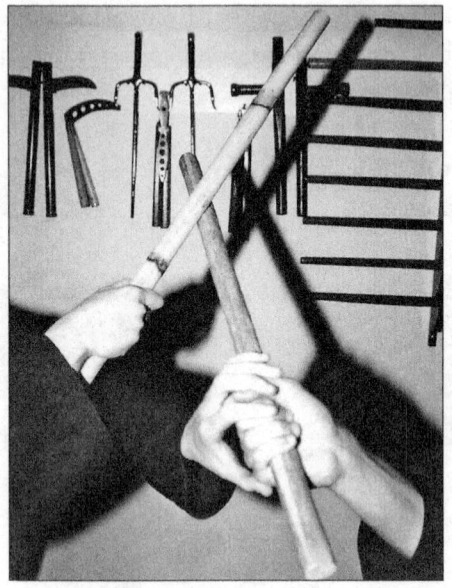

Block-check-counter: parrying and counter-striking.

After blocking a downward strike,
the defender flows into a disarming technique.

- **His sense of humor:**

In 1996 there was an intensive four-day arnis camp held on a New England college campus. It was hot and the training was rigorous. In a late evening session, my partner's cane, slick with sweat, slipped ever so slightly, and cracked across my knuckles. For a moment, my hand went numb, causing the tip of my cane to drop downward sharply, coming to rest in the vicinity of my partner's groin.

The next day at breakfast, Professor Presas noticed the bandage on my finger. "What happened," he asked with genuine concern? "Chris hit me in the finger," I replied, nodding across the table at my friend. "In fairness," Chris added, "Peter then hit me in the groin…" The Professor considered this for a moment, and then said to Chris with a wry grin: "in that case, you lose."

- **His last major seminar:**

In February of 2001 there was a massive, weekend-long arnis gathering in Philadelphia. On the first day, the students, who had come from far and wide, were disappointed to see that it seemed the Professor, who had recently taken ill, would be unable to attend. Nevertheless, they trained hard under the watchful eye of his senior students, and learned a great many things. In the afternoon of the second day, while the air was thick with the smell of smoking wood and clattering sticks, there was a stir in the vicinity of the entrance hall.

Gingerly, the Professor, having escaped from hospital and still showing signs of recent surgery, made his way into the room and surveyed the crowd of happy faces that welcomed him. All motion stopped. One by one, he greeted each familiar face. When he got to me, he seemed to look right through me, and simply murmured, "hello Steve." I was heartbroken, but smiled back, and said, "hello Professor."

In time, the training resumed, and the Professor was escorted to a chair on the side of the proceedings. After a few minutes, the training was again brought to a sudden halt, this time by the Professor's booming voice: "Peter!" I looked over, unsure how to react. A few of the senior students surrounding him beckoned me over. When I got to him, he took my hand and said, "I am sorry—I did not recognize you—my eyesight, it is not so good right now." Even in this critical condition, it was important to him to make sure that my feelings were not hurt—that was simply the type of gentleman he was.

- **An image:**

As all of his students know, the Professor was a man of few words, honoring the martial arts dictum, "show, don't say." As a result, a written retrospective can hardly do his memory justice. Images we will always remember—the

Professor's wide, open smile; the twinkle in his eye when he was playing a joke, or just feeling happy; on more serious occasions "making *mano*"—the Filipino sign of respect executed by placing the back of the hand to the forehead—these speak more eloquently of the grace and character of the man than words could ever convey.

- **On taking time to smell the roses:**

While being driven to the seminar described at the outset of this chapter, the Professor suddenly exclaimed, "stop the car!" Concerned that perhaps he was feeling unwell I complied immediately. The car skidded to a halt on the shoulder, spraying up gravel and dust, and causing a few passing drivers to honk angrily. No sooner had we come to a halt than the Professor leapt out, and jogged back about a hundred yards on the highway, stopping at the verge of a meadow.

After a moment, I followed, to see if anything was the matter. Upon drawing near, it became clear what it was that had caught his attention. In the middle of the field was a lone cherry tree, radiant in glorious blossom. A minute passed in silence. Then the Professor announced, "it is beautiful," and trotted back to the car as though nothing unusual had happened. Perhaps for him, it hadn't.

- **The final days:**

A few days before he died, the Professor called my home in Harrisburg from his hospital room in Victoria, wanting to speak to my wife and me. Over the course of about half an hour, we chatted about this and that—nothing very remarkable. He sounded lucid and happy, but at the end of this, our last conversation, he said to us, "I love you, you know…"

We love you too Professor, we miss you, and we hope that wherever you are, there are at least a few cherry trees.

The author with Professor Presas
at a seminar conducted at the
University of Pennsylvania, circa 1995.

chapter 7

# Pirates of the Philippines:
# A Critical Thinking Exercise

by Ruel A. Macaraeg, M.A., J.D.

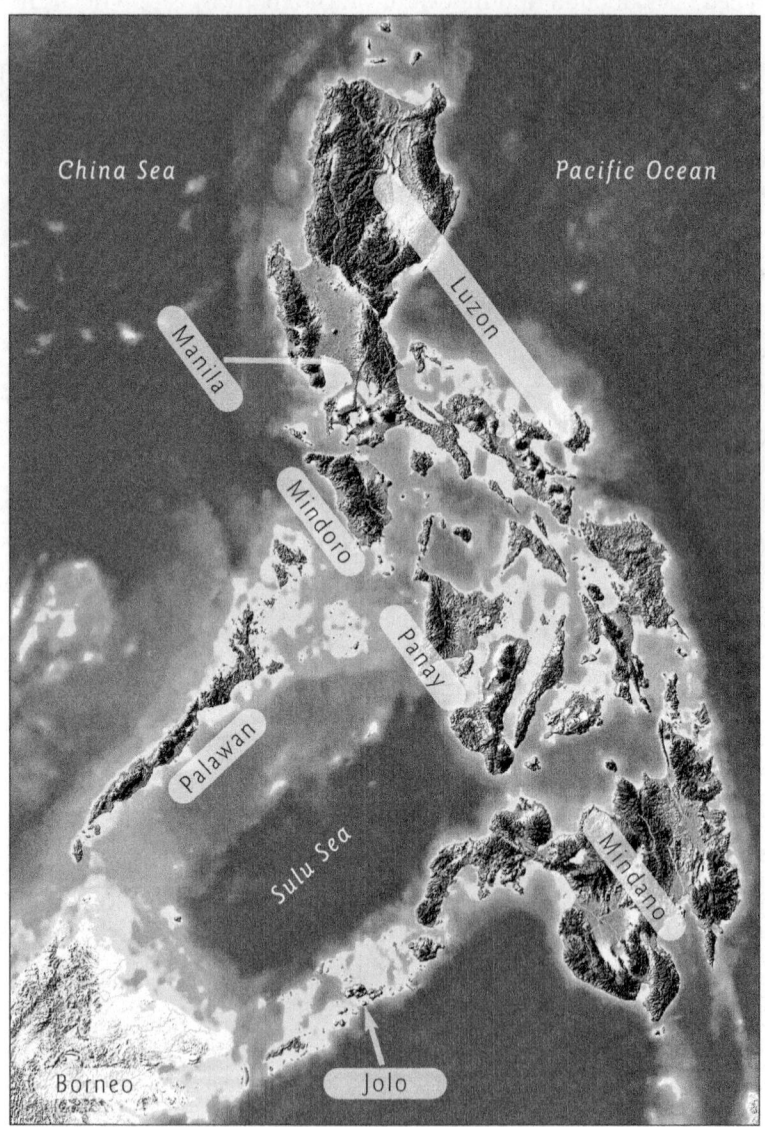

## Philippine Islands
The sea routes in and around the Philippines contain numerous small islands ideal for hiding small warships conducive for pirate activities and a mixing of martial traditions.

# Introduction

Pirates, of late, have sailed back into the public consciousness, both in fiction (with the blockbuster *Pirates of the Caribbean* franchise) and fact (off the Somali coast). One positive result of this interest has been to draw academic attention to historical piracy, even if most of that effort is to deconstruct popular misconceptions. The time seems right, then, to turn a critical eye toward the neglected Moro pirates of the southern Philippines. In their day, these pirates—like their better known Caribbean counterparts—shaped economies and altered national policies across a wide region as communities reacted to their depredations. No history of the Philippines is complete without considering their impact, yet they tend to receive scant mention in published sources. Even stranger is the neglect shown by writers on Filipino martial arts (FMA). Ranging across the whole of oceanic Southeast Asia, these pirates were certainly the primary transmitters of bladed combat as they encountered a diversity of martial cultures and incorporated many foreign elements into their crews (as, again, Caribbean, Barbary, and Japanese pirates are known to have done).

The present discussion is an attempt to amend the record. We begin by clarifying the relevant terms "Moro" and "pirate." As will be seen, much of the confusion stems from misapplication of these imprecise designations. Next, we apply these concepts to investigate the nature of pirate combat generally, and its constraints within the context of the mid- and late-colonial Philippines and the contemporaneous Moro sultanates. These constraints will help us identify the clothing and weapons specific to the pirates as distinguished from both other pirates and other Filipinos. Finally, we conclude by applying these findings toward a reevaluation of the historiography of FMA—its forms, practices, and values.

## "Moros," "Pirates," and "Moro Pirates"

Originally applied by Spaniards to Muslim Moors of North African Arab and Berber origin, "Moro" was transferred to newly encountered Muslims during Far Eastern expeditions in the sixteenth century (Che Man, 1990: 22). This exonym implied a cultural homogeneity that seems not to have existed at the time, and indeed when war erupted between the Philippine colonial government and the Moros in the 1630s, it required significant effort to unify the latter against this external threat (Wiley, 1996: 45-46; McKenna, 1998: ch. 3-4). The failure of the Spanish conquest led to a general peace that belies the image of mutual and continuous holy war presented in FMA writing.

What did persist, though, was piracy by Iranun Moros against colonial Philippine settlements and other coastal targets throughout the Malay-Indonesian Archipelago (McKenna, 1998: 31, 74-75; Wallace, 1890: 261). While other Moros confined their hostilities with the Spanish and Filipinos to the mid-1600s, the Iranun engaged in continuous raiding for slaves and plunder. This irregular warfare, rather than formal state-level military engagement, had the more lasting impact on patterns of Muslim-Catholic conflict. Over the long term, the "Moro" contribution to traditional FMA has been informed more by the predatory sea raider than the noble battlefield warrior.

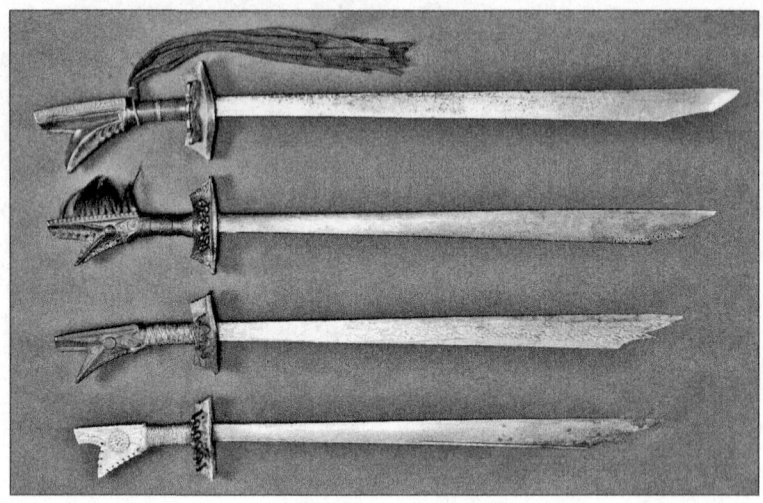

**Kampilan Swords**

Top to bottom: 19th century battle kampilan. Simple in detail, but of very fine hard wood with beautiful grain; Classic 19th century battle kampilan; 19th century kampilan with a rare pattern welded damascus blade; Rare 18th/19th century whale bone handle kampilan for a person of high status or wealth. *Photograph courtesy of www.EriksEdge.com*

Yet despite the obviousness of this conclusion, the piracy aspect of Moro fighting was again overshadowed by the battlefield, thanks to the dramatic Maguindanao and Tausug resistance to American colonization from 1902 through the 1920s (Linn, 2000: 225-231; Che Man, 1990: 46-61; de Quesada and Walsh, 2007: passim). The Americans inherited and perpetuated the collective Moro exonym, failing again to appreciate the unique Iranun pirate dimensions of martial culture in this region.

The scholarly literature on piracy distinguishes it from (or subdivides it into) variations such as buccaneerism, privateering, or corsair-ship (see, for instance, Konstam, 1999; Konstam and McBride, 2000; Ramila 2009). While recognizing them as valid, we will not observe such distinctions here as the Iranun pirate phenomenon seems to share features of all of these activities and the present short discussion does not permit us to probe the details anyway. For our purposes, we use "piracy" in the general sense of violent predatory banditry carried out by naval and/or amphibious operations for the purpose of seizing commodities. This broad definition allows us to speak collectively of the many forms of Iranun action, from coastal raiding against villages to high-seas engagements against merchant ships.

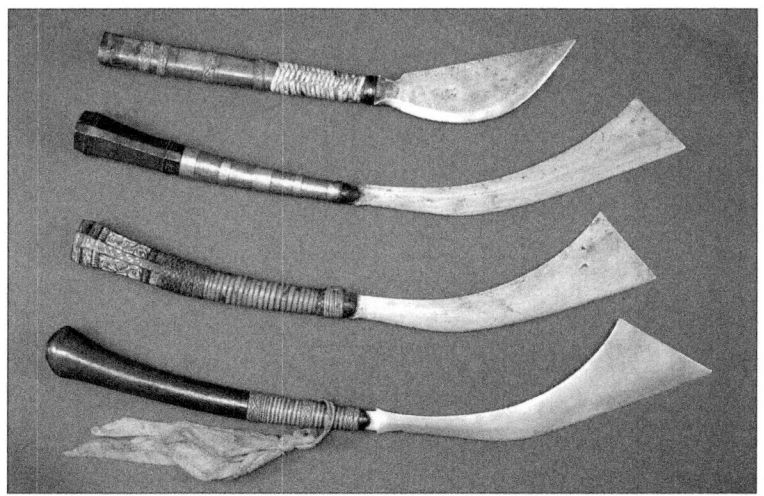

### Panabas

Top to bottom: Small 19th century battle axe panabas with unusually short blade; 19th century panabas with copper and silver bands on the handle; 19th century panabas with rattan wrap and carved designs on the handle; A large 19th century panabas with exaggerated proportions going from thin near the handle to very wide at the tip. *Photograph courtesy of www.EriksEdge.com*

Having now recognized the distinct pirate component within FMA, we now consider what qualitative differences pirate-centered martial arts might have *vis-à-vis* those developed on and intended for the battlefield or street fight.

## The Scope of Pirate Combat and the Context of Filipino Piracy

Like other predatory crimes, piracy arises from motive and opportunity. Rarely have the two been in such ample and consistent supply as in the islands of Southeast Asia; the sea route connects major population concentrations in the Far East and India, and is itself abundant with natural resources. Along the way are sprinkled thousands of small islands ideal for hiding small warships, and many of these islands have rivers winding through jungles upward toward defensible villages in the mountains. Not surprisingly, the Iranun were simply one of a long series of pirate brethren operating in the area—Malays, Bugis, and

Dayaks were indigenous, while larger Chinese, Japanese, Tamil, and Dutch fleets were attracted from beyond. The situation here compares very similarly to the Caribbean and Aegean, two other commercially trafficked archipelagos historically infested with pirates (Konstam, 1991: passim).

Specifically, the Iranun "Golden Age of Piracy" was stimulated by a perfect storm of political conditions. The late seventeenth century détente between the Spanish Philippines and Moro Sultanates, together with the Dutch United East Indian Company suppression of Bugis piracy (Spruit, 1995: 91-95) and Chinese Qing Dynasty's (1644-1911) suppression of Sino-Japanese piracy (Struve, 1993: ch. 12-13) at the same time, meant that profitable shipping once more resumed, now magnified by trans-Pacific American commerce. The emergence of a safe Moro port at Jolo, capital of the Sulu Sultanate, was supported by British agents determined to undermine Spanish interests (McKenna, 1998: 78-79). With the previous generation of pirates eliminated, others moved in to fill the vacuum. One such population was the Moros around Lake Ranao (Lanao) in Mindanao; it appears that this period saw the divergence of the Iranun ("those from Ranao") from the Maranao ("those of Ranao") as the former moved to the coast and took up piracy, eventually settling as far west as Sabah in northeast Borneo (Hamilton, ed. 1998: 64). The Iranun enjoyed great success in their predations until the mid-1800s, when for the first time Spanish ships under steam could effectively pursue them (McKenna, 1998: 78). British colonials in the Malay States did the same against Riau Lanun (Gwin and Stanmeyer, 2007: 132-133; Spruit, 1995: 114) and Dayak (Knight and Scollins, 1990: 20) pirates.

As with all pirates, Iranun objectives were to seize portable wealth, in the form of tangible products and slaves, and sell it at market in Jolo and Maguindanao. In martial arts terms, this meant developing a panoply of light skirmish weapons which would not encumber a fighter either aboard ship or during disembarkation as he rushed ashore to sack a coastal village. Thus, we would expect to find short swords as the preferred weapons, and indeed we see exactly this in the cutlasses of contemporaneous Caribbean buccaneers and pirates. Several forms of Moro cutlass make the case for convergent evolution in pirate swordsmanship. While not confined to pirate combat, these cutlasses can hardly have been improved upon for that purpose: A *barong* or *kris* would be more than adequate to subdue most coastal fishers and farmers.

This helps to explain FMA's focus on short swords, something hitherto inadequately explained by commentators who assume a battlefield origin for these arts. Just as pirates would favor cutlasses, their targets, if armed at all, would have their *bolos* (machete-like tools) of comparable length and shape. Unlike the contexts fostering other Asian martial arts, the violence between Iranun and Spanish-Filipinos was more irregular than military and their choice of arms reflects this. We now turn to other differences in weapons and costume to further explore the pirate contribution to Filipino martial culture.

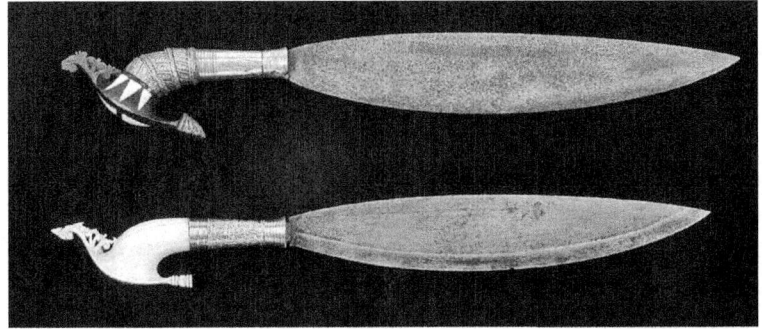

### Barong
*Photograph courtesy of www.EriksEdge.com*

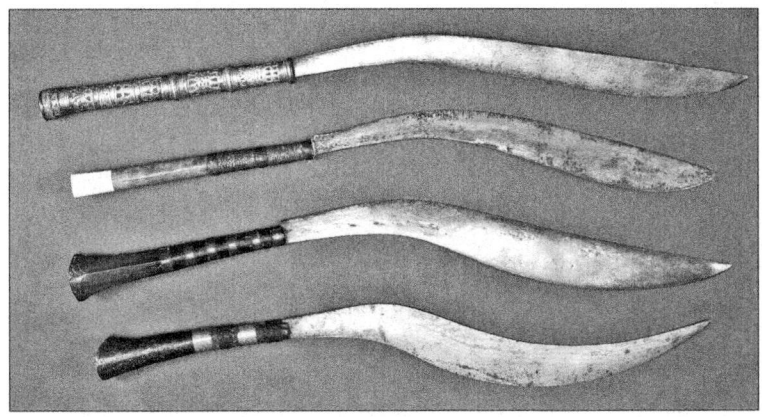

### Panabas
Top to bottom: 19th century double-edged panabas with intricate bronze collar over the handle; 19th century panabas with double-edged blade, woven brass wire and a bone end cap; a very large and heavy 19th century double-edged panabas; a rare 19th century panabas with concave and convex blade that is sharp on both sides. *Photograph courtesy of www.EriksEdge.com*

## Pirates Dressed and Armed

The author has encountered few direct sources of evidence for Iranun pirate dress and armament; nonetheless, much can be inferred from later Moro sources, literary works, and comparison with other pirates in the Southeast Asian sphere. An 1848 woodcut (reproduced in Hamilton, 1998: 136) shows a cannon-mounted Iranun *prahu* ship and its crew, who wear trousers, chemises, vests, sarongs, and turbans—roughly comparable to other maritime people of the region. Several spears and at least one cutlass (probably a *kris*, tucked into the waist of one pirate) are seen. A lithograph from the same source (reproduced Id.: 137; Warren, 2002, inside cover) shows a "Malay chief" from Jolo similarly attired, with two *krisses* clearly shown tucked, again, at the waist. A third illustration shows a posture similar to the one previous, with spear held upright and *kris* again tucked at the waist. This pirate, unlike the others, does not wear an under-layer of chemise and trousers, wearing only a sleeveless vest and sarong with his turban. He and several of the *prahu* pirates, in contrast to the Jolo illustration, are shown with a length of cloth fastened as a chinstrap over the turban, and this may be to secure a small helmet or arming cap not clearly visible from the artwork.

**Prahu Ship**

Illustration adapted from: Marryat, F. (1848). *Borneo and the Indian archipelago*. London: Longman, Brown, Green, and Longmans, Paternoster-Row. www.gutenberg.net

While armor is known among the Moros and was used by Maguindanao as recently as the early 20th century American wars (Robinson, 1960; Wiley, 1996: 130; Stone, 1934: s.v. "Armor"), we have no evidence of it for the Iranun. This is expected, since such armor would slow down men and small ships on the move.

Konstam (1999: 184-185) points out how Caribbean pirates wore clothing typical of seamen at the time, which contrasted with landsmen's but was otherwise not specific to them in their capacity as brigands. This appears to have been the case as well with Iranun pirates—clothing was pragmatic and comfortable, and indistinguishable from that of other sailors. If the three images above are indicative, we notice that in contrast to land-dwelling Moros and other related peoples, the pirates did not seem to have expensive brocaded or ikat woven fabric. This is consistent with the author's global survey of armed fashion (Macaraeg, 2007), which revealed a pattern of use for expensive clothing in conjunction with personal arms only in contexts where interpersonal violence was to be avoided. As status indicators, such clothing carried associations of relative social status and access to power which could deter spontaneous violence. Since spontaneous violence was the entire point behind piracy, these semiotics were unnecessary for the Iranun and they dressed in what we might jokingly call "business casual."

**Cannon**
18th century Moro bronze cannon "Lantaka".

Cutlasses as described above were certainly the mainstay of Iranun sword fighting. Aside from attacking shore-bound targets, short blades were ideal for boarding actions. Caribbean pirate scholars have repeatedly explained the advantages of short cutters in the confines of a shipboard fight (Breverton, 2004: 43; Konstam and McBride, 1998: 12; Little, 2005: 67-69). More difficult to explain are the longer *kampilan* swords said to be "favored" by Iranun (Demetrio, 1991, v2: 592), with overall lengths approaching or exceeding 1 meter (1.094 yards). Like other full-length swords, they require more space for movement and footwork than cutlasses to be used effectively. Would pirates have had need for such a weapon?

Again, we can look to contemporaneous Euro-Caribbean and Sino-Japanese pirates for analogues. A number of 17th and 18th century illustrations show buccaneer and pirate captains brandishing cross- and basket-hilt broadswords, of comparable length to *kampilans* (see, passim, Konstam and McBride, 1998 and 2000, for reproduced illustrations). Japanese and Chinese sabers also have lengths of roughly 1 meter. One reasonable possibility for needing these longer blades is an anticipation of encountering regular Spanish soldiers armed with swords of their own. Though no longer pursuing an active expansionist agenda under Bourbon administration, Spanish troops were still formidable fighters as shown in their successful suppression of numerous revolts in the Philippines and throughout the Americas (Weber, 2005). Outside the Philippines, other and better-armed native coastal settlements may also have had war swords; an illustration of warriors from Gorontalo (northern Sulawesi) shows them armed with *kampilans* of their own (Racinet, 1988: 48-49). Iban Dayaks of Sarawak had swords very similar to *kampilan*, and even more similar were Timorese swords, which even had the distal spike so characteristic of *kampilan* blade tips (Zonneveld, 2002: s.v. "Swords of the Timor Group"). Both of these latter peoples, victims of early Iranun raids, eventually joined Moro crews as some of their most effective fighters (Warren, 2002: 111ff).

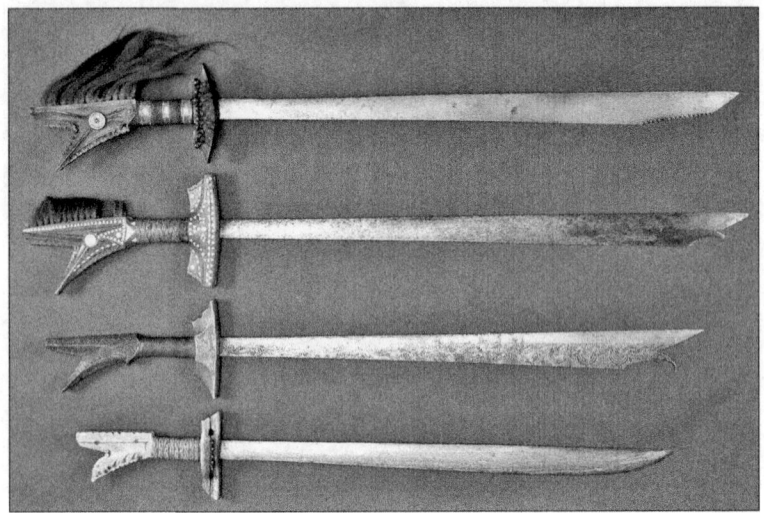

**Kampilan**

Top to bottom: A great 19th century battle kampilan with double guard and red hair; 19th century presentation kampilan with mother of pearl inlay on the handle; 19th century presentation kampilan with chiseled design on the blade; a rare 18th/19th century whale bone handle Moro kampilan for a person of high status or wealth. *Photograph courtesy of www.EriksEdge.com*

At this point we should pause to mention a claim attached to *kampilans* that is certainly false: That their scabbards were bound with thin lashing to enable a faster draw because the blade would simply cut through the lashing (Stone, 1934: 160; Wiley, 1996: 119; Evangelista, 1995: 88). A moment's critical reflection reveals that one would still need to apply pressure to the lashings in a direction away from one's intended target, which would retard rather than quicken a draw. Further, such pressure would need to be applied against a resisting force, and we have no evidence that *kampilans* were suspended by straps or baldrics (and then, wouldn't the sword need to cut through those too?). We observe from Japanese *iaijutsu* that the fastest and most effective way to attack on the draw is simply to unsheathe the blade according to technique specific to that purpose. Cato (1996) relates that *kampilans* were probably stored in arsenals or ships' hulls, to be distributed before an attack. We may note the similarity to Japanese *wako* who appear, from period illustrations, to have done the same with their *katanas*, since they are rarely shown wearing sword scabbards (Turnbull and Hook, 2007: 28).

Another weapon attributed to the Iranun but without clear analogues among other pirates is the chopper called *panabas* or *tabas*. The comment that it was used by older or weaker warriors to finish off wounded enemies in battle (Demetrio, 1991, v2: 596) is unconvincing. The *prahu*, like any fighting vessel, could not afford to be hindered by the presence of old or weak crewmen. (And anyway, why assign the heaviest weapons to the weakest sailors?) The liability would be even more evident during raids which depended on stealth and speed. The record indicates that Iranun piracy does not appear to have involved large-scale battles in the formal sense, as might describe the Chinese pirate attacks on Pangasinan in 1572 (Harper and Peplow, 1991: 191) and Manila in 1574 (Wiley, 1996: 44). If at all, Iranun would most likely have used choppers to cut rigging, making them analogous to rigging axes on contemporaneous Western ships. Finally, we can mention the spears alluded to in the illustrations discussed above; they are clearly analogous to Western boarding pikes.

**FMA Historiography: A Re-Assessment**

Acknowledging the Iranun pirates' role in shaping Filipino combative culture poses problems for the received tradition of FMA values. FMA is a product of Filipino national consciousness, itself a recent cultural construction —the label intentionally subordinates cultural heterogeneity to the needs of synthetic political identity. An invented national ethos can only arise from a national story—a historiography—which binds its members through a shared sense of collective historical experience. FMA has provided that story: Of a native people who heroically endured centuries of foreign oppression, faithfully preserving their original battlefield (i.e. "Moro") fighting skills in sublimated stick and knife forms until opportunity (and Americans) presented them with the chance to rise up and assert independence.

In reality, FMA has been fundamentally shaped by the experience of Iranun piracy. Rather than national unity, the collective martial experience of the Philippines is largely one of internal, native-on-native raiding, with little of the romanticized glory achieved on battlefields elsewhere in Asia. Those wanting to accurately understand historical Filipino combatives must come to terms with the unpleasant reality of piracy. To do so is not to diminish the skill or ingenuity evident in kali, arnis, or eskrima, but rather to accept them for what they, as all true martial arts, are—techniques to achieve personal (and sometimes social) goals by the systematic application of physical violence. Detaching superimposed values from the historical reality of any marital arts can only improve our objectivity and, by extension, our efforts to study and preserve them.

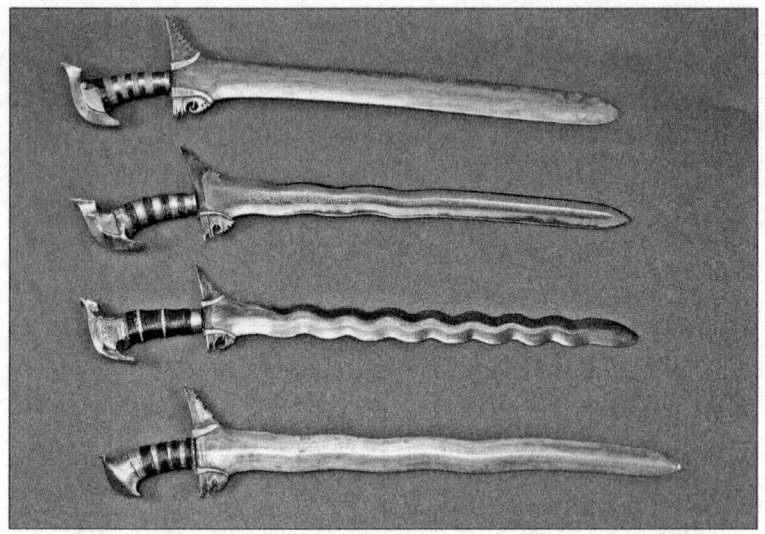

### Kris

Top to bottom: 19th century Moro kris with straight blade and large silver cockatoo handle; 19th century Moro kris with silver cockatoo handle and a half wavy half straight blade with a hollow ground fuller and a silver inlay talisman; 19th century Moro kris with silver cockatoo handle with original fiber handle wrap and very wavy blade; 19th century Moro kris (Mindanao) with cast bronze handle. The blade shows a good pattern and slight shallow waves.

This is not to say that martial artists today should study their arts in an ethical vacuum. Rather, we simply must resist the urge to reinvent the past in order to satisfy our modern cultural romanticisms. If the martial arts teach us anything, it is that we can act to take control of our personal circumstances, which includes the ability to stand on our own without having to rely on the reputations of our forebears to validate the legitimacy of who we are and what we practice.

**Special Thanks to Erik Farrow**
for the photographs used to help illustrate this chapter.
He is a seller of authentic antique swords, arms and
shields from around the world. www.EriksEdge.com

## References

Breverton, T. (2004). *The pirate dictionary*. Gretna, LA: Pelican Publishing.

Che Man, W. (1990). *Muslim separatism: The Moros of southern Philippines and the Malays of southern Thailand*. Singapore: Oxford University Press.

Clements, J. (1997). *Renaissance swordsmanship*: The illustrated book of rapiers and cut and thrust swords and their use. Boulder, CO: Paladin Press.

Cole, M., Connolly, P., Spring, C., Harding, A., and Wilkinson, F. (1993). *Swords and hilt weapons*. New York: Barnes & Noble.

de Quesada, A., and Walsh, S. (2007). *The Spanish-American War and Philippine insurrection 1898-1902*. Oxford, UK: Osprey Publishing.

Demetrio, F. (1991). *Encyclopedia of Philippine folk beliefs and customs. Volume 2: Folk medicine to weaponry*. Cagayan de Oro City, R.P.: Xavier University.

Evangelista, N. (1995). *The encyclopedia of the sword*. Santa Barbara, CA: Greenwood.

Gwyn, P., and Stanmeyer, J. (2007). Dark passage: The strait of Malacca. *National Geographic, 212*(4) p. 126-149.

Hamilton, R. (ed.) (1998). *From the rainbow's varied hue: Textiles from the southern Philippines*. Los Angeles, CA: University of California Press.

Harper, P., and Peplow, E. (1991). *Philippines handbook*. Berkeley, CA: Avalon Travel Publishing.

Knight, I., and Scollins, R. (1990). *Queen Victoria's enemies (4): Asia, Australasia and the Americas*. Oxford, UK: Osprey Publishing.

Konstam, A. (1999). *The history of pirates*. Guilford, CT: Lyons Press.

Konstam, A., and McBrid, A. (1998). *Pirates 1660-1730*. Oxford, UK: Osprey Publishing.

Konstam, A., and McBride, A. (2000). *Buccaneers 1620-1700*. Oxford, UK: Osprey Publishing.

Linn, B. (2000). *The Philippine War 1899-1902*. Lawrence, KS: University Press of Kansas.

Little, B. (2005). *The sea rover's practice: Pirate tactics and techniques, 1630-1730*. Dulles, VA: Potomac Books.

Macaraeg, R. (2007 March). Dressed to kill: Toward a theory of fashion in arms and armor. *Fashion Theory: The Journal of Dress, Body, & Culture* v11 (1): 41-64.

McKenna, T. (1998). *Muslim rulers and rebels: Everyday politics and armed separatism in the southern Philippines*. Los Angeles, CA: University of California Press.

Racinet, A. (1988). *The historical encyclopedia of costume*. New York: Checkmark Books.

Robinson, H. (1967). *Oriental armor*. New York: Walker and Co.

Spruit, R. (1995). *The land of the sultans: An illustrated history of Malaysia*. Amsterdam: Pepin Press.

Stone, G. (1934/1999). A glossary of the construction, decoration and use of arms and armor. Mineola, NY: Dover Publications.

Struve, L. (Tran., Ed.) (1993). *Voices from the Ming-Qing cataclysm: China in tigers' jaws*. New Haven, CT: Yale University Press.

Wallace, A. (1890/2000). *The Malay archipelago*. North Clarendon, VT: Periplus Editions.

Weber, D. (2005). *Barbaros: Spaniards and their savages in the age of enlightenment*. New Haven, CT: Yale University Press.

Wiley, M. (1996). *Filipino martial culture*. Boston: Tuttle Publishing.

Woodard, C. (2009 Spring). Quelling a pirate revolt. *MHQ: The Quarterly Journal of Military History, 21*(3): 8-19.

chapter 8

# A Few Favored Modern Arnis Techniques

by Ken Smith

## Where I Learned These Techniques

The two techniques I've selected as favorites are the center lock with cane, and a technique we'll simply refer to as "left-hand technique number 1." I practiced and refined these techniques under the tutelage of the late Grandmaster Remy Presas. But my initial introduction to each of these techniques came at the hands of other arnisadors: center lock with cane was introduced to me by his first arnis teacher, George Mazek, although it was not until sometime later that I came to appreciate the full power of this technique. Likewise, it was Chuck Gauss who first introduced me to left-hand technique number 1, which many people recognize as Professor Presas's go-to technique in almost any situation. As a result, it is fair to say that this second technique was a favorite of Gauss as well.

## Memorable Incidents Involving These Techniques

One of the wonderful things about having the opportunity to train directly with the headmaster of a system is being able to learn by feeling. Every student can see the master performing the technique and hear his verbal instructions, but only the student with whom the technique is being demonstrated can actually feel the move. This experience serves to convey nuances that simply elude detection by the other senses. In this respect, I was fortunate to be a favorite choice of partner for Professor Presas when demonstrating a technique. And while I had learned the center lock with cane some time before, it was not until a seminar in Michigan with Professor Presas in the early 1990s that I experienced its full effect. Rather than simply induce localized pain in my wrist, the application of the lock by Professor Presas—while not unduly rough—caused a shock reaction that extended beyond his wrist, affecting my entire body. This kind of hands-on experience provides lessons of incomparable value for those who strive to attain true mastery of their chosen art.

One of the most important teachings in any martial art is that techniques must be performed with the right mind-set. This is especially important when dealing with set-up techniques, fakes, or feints. Unless the opponent truly believes the initial move is being executed in earnest, he will not be drawn into the behavior it is intended to elicit. Worse still, if the opponent recognizes the feint as a hollow threat, he will have a window to launch his own attack with impunity.

It will, in essence, give him a free shot. With this teaching in mind, one of the more memorable aspects of performing left-hand technique number 1 is the way in which the initial counter—while planned to set up for the next move—will often reach its target unchecked if the opponent is not quick and alert, thereby obviating the need for the rest of the sequence. In this way, the set-up technique may actually become the finishing technique if executed with the proper mind-set.

**Tips on Practicing the Center Lock with Cane**
- When performing the center lock with cane, the practitioner should employ a "tapi-tapi block." Unlike the more basic "post block," where the defender blocks using his cane but braces it on the rear side with his palm, in executing the tapi-tapi block, the cane blocks the cane and the arm blocks the arm.
- When the opponent attacks, the defender must ensure that the angle of his cane matches the angle of the striking cane, otherwise the canes may miss one another.
- Similarly, in executing the cane block, the defender must avoid crossing the centerline with his weapon. Failing to follow this rule may cause the block to make contact but then collapse.
- When the defender grasps his opponent's cane, his pinky finger should touch the opponent's thumb so he can detect his opponent's grip by feel.

**Tips on Practicing Left-Hand Technique Number 1**
- In performing left-hand technique number 1, it is important to note that after executing a tapi-tapi block in response to his opponent's strike, the defender counters not just with the right backfist, but also with a simultaneous left jab to the opponent's stomach with the tip of the cane. This additional, simultaneous attack is easy to miss if you are not looking for it.
- After the opponent accepts the "invitation" to parry the backfist and goes to strike the defender with his cane a second time, the defender must step forward and out to the side with his left leg in order to "counter the counter" effectively. This footwork will reorient the angle of engagement, creating a new centerline for the defender while forcing the attacker to cross his own centerline, thereby weakening him enough to allow the defender's (grabbed) right arm to overpower the opponent's left (grabbing) arm.

## TECHNIQUE 1: Center Lock with Cane

1a) The attacker backhand strikes at shoulder level with a cane. 1b) The defender blocks with his own cane and controls the attacking arm with his left hand. 1c) The defender slides his empty hand onto his opponent's cane and pulls it toward himself while striking at the opponent's ear with the butt end of his own cane, inviting the opponent to parry. 1d) When the opponent parries, the defender pushes the opponent's cane tip down over the opponent's wrist, and locks it in place with his cane. He then pins the opponent's open hand on his wrist to apply the center lock. 1e) The defender finishes with a strike to the face while bracing the opponent's head with his other hand.

## TECHNIQUE 2: Left-Hand Technique Number 1

2a) The attacker strikes at shoulder level with his cane. 2b) The defender blocks the strike with his cane and controls the opponent's hand with his right hand. 2c) The defender immediately strikes with a right backfist to the attacker's head, inviting a block while the tip of his cane simultaneously strikes the opponent's stomach. 2d) The attacker parries the backfist down and retracts his cane to strike again. 2e) The defender changes his stance and angle, forcing the attacker to cross his centerline. He parries the attacker's second strike, and counterstrikes to his head to end the sequence.

# index

*Advanced Balisong*, 15
Agrippa, Camillo, 8-9
angles of attack, 9, 13, 71
armor, 8, 56-57, 64, 67, 69, 100,
arnis, 2, 13-14, 22-24
*Arnis De Mano*, 15
Arnis Fernandez, 39
*Arnis: Filipino Art of Stick Fighting*, 15
Arnis Lanada, 39
Arnis Pangasinan, 25, 39
Arnis Tendencia , 39
Ateneo de Manila, 12
Bacon, Venancio, 13
Balintawak Cuentada, 13, 25, 39
barong, 24, 57-61, 98-99
Bataugong (Chief), 4
Biñas, Herminia B., 14-15
Biñas Dynamic Arnis, 15
blow gun, 2, 24
*Book on the Greatness of the Sword*, 10
*Book on the Philosophy of Arms*, 10
bow and arrow, 2, 24
Cabales, Angel, 14
Cabalas Serrada Escrima, 14, 25, 38, 86
Caballero, Jose, 14
Cañete, Ciriaco, 15-16, 39
cannon, 4, 99, 101
Cinco Tero Eskrima, 20
*Complete Teachings of the Old Fencers*, 7
dagger, 2, 4, 8, 11-12, 14, 27, 85
de Campo Uno-Dos-Tres Original, 14
de Carranza, Jeronimo, 9-10
De Fondo Escrima, 39
death-matches, 25, 31, 33-34
di Grassi, Giacomo, 8
Diego, Tony, 26
Dillman, George, 86-87
*Doce Pares: Basic Arnis, Eskrima, Pangolisi*, 15
Escorpizo, Oonfre C., 20, 39
Escrido, 16, 39
eskrima, 2, 4, 6, 8-9, 11-14, 16, 22-24, 70
Estalilla, Ramiro U., Sr., 20, 39
Fernandez, Nes, 39

*The Filipino Martial Arts*, 15
Fong, Leo, 86
Galang, Reynaldo S., 39
Gaus, Chuck, 107
Geronimo, Jimmy, 30-31
Geronimo, Meliton C., 39
Giron, Leo M., 39
grappling arts, 22-23, 44
Hagibis, 15, 23-25, 39
helmet, 56, 68, 100
*His True Arte of Defence*, 8
Ilustrisimo, Antonio, 15, 25-26, 39
Inosanto, Dan, 15
Japanese influence, 16, 24, 37
Jay, Wally, 86
kalasag (shield), 10, 65-67
kali, 1-4, 10-14, 16 note 1, 17 note 6, 22-24, 44
Kali Ilustrisimo, 14-15, 26, 39
kampilan (cutlass), 10, 20, 24, 57-59, 96, 101-103
klewang (sword), 63
*Knowledge in the Art of Arnis*, 15
komedya plays, 2, 11
kris, 24, 61-62, 98, 100, 104
kuntao, 4, 23, 55
Kuntao Lima-lima, 28-29, 39
Lamay, Bantug, 4
Lameco Eskrima, 15, 25, 39
Lañada, Carlito A., 15, 28-29, 39, 43-45, 55
Lañada, Porferio S., 15, 39
langka-silat, 1, 22
Lapu Lapu (king), 4, 10
Lebkommer, Hans, 7
Lightning Scientific Arnis System, 15, 27, 39
Luna Lema, Benjamin, 15, 27, 39
Magellan, Ferdinand, 1, 4, 10-11, 17 note 3
Mangal (Datu), 4
Maranga, Timoteo, 14
Mariñas, Amante P., Sr., 14-15, 39
Marozzo, Achille, 8
Mazek, George, 107
migrations, 2-4
Modern Arnis, 15-16, 39, 87, 89, 107-110

*Modern Arnis: Filipino Art of Stick Fighting*, 15
Pacheco y Narvaez, Luis, 9
panabas, 64, 97, 99, 103
Pananandata, 14, 39
pencak-silat, 1, 22
personal styles, 4, 15, 22, 25
piracy, 95-98, 101, 103-104
poison, 2, 57
prahu ship, 100, 103
Presas, Remy A., 15-16, 39, 83-93, 107
provincial styles, 15, 25
rebellions, 11-12
Ricketts, Christopher, 26, 39
Rigonan-Estalilla Kabaroan, 20, 24, 39
Rizal y Mercado, Jose, 12
Sagasa kickboxing, 15, 23, 25, 39
*The Secrets of Arnis*, 15
shield, 2, 7, 10, 56, 64-68
Shito-ryu, 55
Shorin-ryu, 55
Sikaran, 23-24, 30-31, 39
spear, 2, 4, 10, 56, 66, 100, 103
Sulite, Edgar G., 15, 39
sword and dagger (espada y daga), 8, 12, 14, 25
Taboada, Bobby, 39
taming (shield), 65
tapi-tapi, 85, 108
Tendencia, Samson, 39
Terry, Charles, 86-87
Tobosa, Raymond, 3, 39
Tobosa Kali/Escrima, 39
training stages of escrima, 13
Tres Personas Arnis, 14
tribal chiefton (datu), 3-4, 16 note 1, 61
Umpad, Sonny, 70
Vee Arnis-jitsu, 1, 15, 25, 39
Visayan Corto Kadena Eskrima, 70-71
Visitacion, Florendo M., 1, 39
war dance, 3, 17 note 2, 32, 46
World War II, 14, 43, 57, 64
wrestling (buno), 1, 24, 32
Yambao, Placido, 14, 16 note 1